FORSAKEN HYMNS

FORSAKEN HYMNS

Thomas Fasano

Coyote Canyon Press
Claremont, California

First Edition

Table of Contents

Forsaken Hymn no. 1

Beneath willow shadows, I pause;
the textured bark whispers memoirs of resilience:
how Archie, spirit cocooned in quiet defiance,
held worlds within, uncharted and sacred,
his laughter—a broken echo over leaves,
those syllables of soul's resistance.

Guarded, he navigated life's physics—
the gravity of expectations,
  the inertia of solitude:
how hearts orbit around common suns,
yet feel the chill of distant planets,
each star a story, burning to reveal.

In the languid air, Archie's essence lingers,
woven through the branches stretching skyward:
  this tapestry of quiet battles and victories
  tells of bearing weight, enduring strain,
  and the art of persisting—
  relief comes as the final leaf falls, serene.

Forsaken Hymn no. 2

In this silent town, streets stretch:
empty scripts, devoid of daybreak's actors.
Every corner turned is a pause in thought,
isolated yet pregnant with echo—
the ghost of chatter, laughter swallowed
by the ordinance of emptiness.

Where once was a pulse, now a flatline:
this quiet, not peace but a muffled scream.
Nature abhors a vacuum: so do souls.
Our once boisterous playground,
now chambers of solitude,
where solitude is not sought but imposed.

Yet in this starkness, clarity emerges:
    bare branches against a winter sky,
lessons in the lean lines of inhospitable times.
Every emptiness filled with the potential
for new definitions, new rhythms—
life, finding a way like water: soft, but sure.

Forsaken Hymn no. 3

Beneath scattered leaves, a soft decay:
roots delve deep, seeking whispers
lost to the surface's easy forgetfulness:
in this quiet burial, life stirs—
a slow, resilient budding
against the tight clutch of earth.

   The microcosm reveals: spores, laden
     with future forests, hinge on mere moisture:
  how fragile the hold of life, waiting
    for the trigger of rain:
each droplet a universe, birthing
       fields from the void: endless cycle.

   My thoughts, tangled as the underbrush,
sift through the mulch of past seasons:
   in decay and growth, a continuum—
the breath of composted memories
feeding new roots: in this loam,
the seeds of tomorrow find their peace.

Forsaken Hymn no. 4

Echoes within this small square: the universe
spans outward as she reaches for her glass:
our motions are orbital, satellites
circling a common, unseen center:
The clink of ice—faint stars twinkling in sync,
the laugh—soft nebulae blooming in space.
Here, amidst the casual dining cosmos,
her fork a comet, arcing through stardust

of paprika, tracing the orbital paths
defined by the physics of desire.
Our glances—the gravity holding us
in a delicate balance: pull and pause,
wondering which force will prevail.
As she speaks, constellations form
from the words that linger in the warm air,
my thoughts drift to the spaces between stars,

to the quiet dark matter binding us,
the unseen web of longing and restraint.
I ponder the endless dance of particles,
each atom in its place resonating
with the potential of an unknown bond;
the melody of what could be, if only
the universe shifted, aligning our stars.

Forsaken Hymn no. 5

In this hush, a world spins: constellations
drawn in webs, fine as spider silk, catching
dew: each droplet, a miniature lens:
the universe, expanding quietly
within the frame of morning's tender hands,
muscle and sinew of the rooted earth.

    Amid the gauzy vapor of the clouds,
thoughts drift—loose feathers in a vast, blue sea:
  how lightness bears its own form of weight,
    a paradox wrapped in the sky's vast scroll.
Below, mountains shoulder the horizon,
    stalwart, yet inscribed with transience.

And there: the heartbreak of the new, caught
in the dance of leaf against the wind,
an endless cycle of bloom and wither:
creation spins, tightly bound in decay,
each ending cradled in the crook of start:
thus, even in parting, we begin anew.

Forsaken Hymn no. 6

Through the layers of accumulated time,
  I walk: each stone beneath grips,
holds fast the stories of myriad lifetimes,
    chafed and split by ice and sun,
  echoing with the pulse of ceaseless renewal:
how life insists on life, despite the frost.

  Leaves whisper with the tongues of the lost,
outlining minute histories in their decay:
cells breaking down, atoms excited,
violas straining through shriveled scarfs of mulch,
  the grand continuum: our shared breath,
our shared dissolution in the cyclic air.

This path, hardened by the trials of old,
leads not to mere echoes but to voices
that swell in the heartwood of gnarled oak,
deep within the rings, those fibrous tomes:
history not as a burden but a beacon,
a guide: light casting shadows to lead the way.

Forsaken Hymn no. 7

The screen flickers: a continuous cascade
   of light and shadow: epochs slide,
each frame a departure from the last:
how we see not the change but the changing:
   the reel spins, uncatching, always forward:
   beneath this theater, roots of oak spread wide,
understanding, without eyes, the shifting soil,
   absorbing silently the rain's soft lessons:

   how similarly our lives accumulate:
layers upon layers of nuanced growth:
   in the dim glow, I find reflections,
not just on the screen, but beneath,
where the dark holds firm the past's echo:
   thus, in this quiet flicker, I am both viewer and viewed,
witness to the scenes I live and those I have lived through:

locked in this cycle, serene, I comprehend finally.
Beneath the flicker: ancient light,
casting shadows where we sit:
Archie laughs while I, entranced,
struggle to grasp the shifting films,
German, Russian, tales transformed
under the watch of Italian eyes.

Forsaken Hymn no. 8

In this clear, vast sky, they erase:
each layer stripped, a revelation
of bareness beneath the bright sun's gaze,
   where shadows spell the truths of erosion.
The wind's whisper: a clinical slice,
through flesh, through foliage of the soul,
revealing nothing but the ice

of voided spaces, the toll
of their harsh taxonomy.
Yet, in this space of despair,
the seeds of a new being flurry,
   spiral in the breezy air,
drifting to soil where they might marry
light and dark in a fresh narrative,

not imposed but inherently lived.
From destruction blooms the imperative:
to reconstruct, not as I am bid,
    but as I might choose, grains of me
  coalescing in quiet defiance,
    bonding beneath the once-mocking sky's dome.

Forsaken Hymn no. 9

The silence expands between us: all words—
mere vibration, a rustle of leaves through
   withheld breath: my stillness not defiance
    but a gathering, as of storm-drenched air—
her voice cuts through, sharp and crystalline,
   a call to emerge from shadowed corners,
      where roots twine deep into the cool, dark earth,
    and the scent of moss rises—ancient, green.

Above, branches knit a dense web, a shield
    against a slate sky, pulsing with waiting rain:
  here, I stand, pressed into nature's quiet breast,
    my thoughts - sediment settling in clear pools,
and all around, the forest holds its breath,
shifting: a leaf falls, a slow, spiraling descent,
stars push through the night's fabric, pinprick bright.

Am I not also part of this vast weave?
    Interlocked patterns of existence:
the unyielding wood, the resilient leaf,
every element a witness to cycles
  of solitude and the salve of return,
    and so, with her plea echoing, heart-bound,
I step forward, evolved by time's tender hands.

Forsaken Hymn no. 10

In twilight's soft decay, the edges blur:
the day's heat lifts in soft, evaporating sighs,
and there, beneath the spreading chestnut, lies
the shadowed lore of ages, hushed and pure.
Whispers carry through the leaves: messages
from cicada to soil, root to frond:
this constant exchange, life's unbreakable bond,

    coding survival in silent passages.
The world turns, indifferent to its own spinning,
each rotation: a pulse in the vein of time,
connecting atom to cosmos, sublime,
in its indifferent pattern, beginning
    to mirror our own fleeting breaths, equally
lost and found in nature's vast weave, quietly

    resilient—the way sand embraces sea,
and night meets day: transitions, seamlessly.
Yet, within these cycles, a question remains,
etched deep like riverbeds through stone:
   what binds us here, what truly makes us known
is not just the blood's rush but also its pains.

Forsaken Hymn no. 11

The cycles close as the night draws its veil,
each twilight a curtain over the day's end:
our stories weave through time's fabric, frayed
yet held together by the threads of constancy.
Moments are temporary harbors we leave,
   waves lapping at the solidity of our boats,
our sails billow with the winds of change,

each departure a silent echo in the void.
We navigate through the dim starlight,
   searching for the lighthouse of solace:
is peace just another transient wave,
or the deep, unspoken truth beneath?
In the quiet aftermath of departure,
the emptiness is as profound as the sea—

   here, where the heart knows its depths,
and the mind wanders into the infinite.
Continuously arriving and departing,
we inhale beginnings and exhale endings,
finding rhythm in the ceaseless flux,
the pulse of the universe throbbing within.

Forsaken Hymn no. 12

In the half-light where day and dusk mingle,
the secrets of the earth write their whispers
on the underside of newly turned leaves:
each leaf a page, a testament to cycles;
the ancient dance of decay and renewal.
Leaves, crumpled like the hands of aged prophets,
foretell the chill, the inevitable frost

while roots, those subterranean scholars,
gather knowledge in the dark, sipping deep
from the well of shared, silent histories.
I stand, caught in this turning, the pivot
between light's echo and the murmur of night:
the air thick with the scent of musk and myth,
    a lattice of branches reaching, teaching

me the language of the interleaved life.
    A breeze shifts, a soft exhale of the world,
binds me to the breath of fallen timber,
my thoughts adrift on the stream of evening,
where moon and moss conspire in quietude,
painting shadows with the brush of the old.

Forsaken Hymn no. 13

In twilight's deepening, colors bleed:
gold fades to thoughtful blue,
the saffron sky a canvas vast,
    bleeding into dusk's embrace.
    Shadows stretch, merge, lose their edge,
melding as thoughts of Archie do.

His days, a weave of fear and brave,
echo in every human stride:
how he lived, more rat than man,
yet breathed vast human themes,
courage wrapped in fragile skin,
cornered by destiny's wide throw.

Now, as night whispers cold truths,
I, too, wrestle unsure paths,
    our shared humanity, a tangled bond,
    binding us in silent accord.
Beneath the vast indifferent stars,
we stand defiant: Archie, you, I.

Forsaken Hymn no. 14

"Each ripple of grass: a history,"
she murmured: each blade bent by winds
   that traced paths, invisible yet strong,
woven through the fabric of the air: connectivity
  in its purest form, the grass, a green sea:
each wave a silent testimony of persistence.

The sun, too, tells of circular motion:
rising and setting, a tireless reminder
that what fades will return: echoes
   of her words in the gold of dusk,
  the landscape a canvas, where light
draws the contours of infinite returns.

And so, as shadows stretch and the day leans
into night, I find in these repeated motions
a comfort: the unbroken dialogue between
earth and sun, the perpetual loop of cause
and effect: a horizon that promises
the continual bloom of new dawns.

Forsaken Hymn no. 15

Tendrils of smoke: they twist upward,
tracing the narratives of exhausted lives,
each curl a delicate testament to endurance,
vanishing at the touch of outer air,
as if matter, too, knows when to yield
to the vast, uncharted dark.

Below, the streelights throw gold on wet streets:
each raindrop catching glimmer, a brief ignite,
a circuit connecting grime to starlight,
threads of fractured cosmos strewn
on oil-slick puddles: reflecting the episodic burst
of a city pulse, endless, yet bound.

And so we find rhythm, the perennial beat,
woven through our breaths and the spaces between,
our voices carry, dissipate, and somehow sustain
over the constant hum of the gray machine, urban expanse:
in this small, transient symphony, we linger,
complete in our moment, finite yet infinite.

Forsaken Hymn no. 16

In this corner, amidst dust and shadow:
Archie's golden pelt, draped like history
over the chair – silent, still, a testament
to the life that pulsed beneath: vibrant,
unaware of its own temporality, now
a mere exhibit: subtle, admired.

Within these walls, whispers echo,
soft as the brush of fur against skin,
communing with memories once alive,
    now framed: the silent dance of existence
versus the preserved, static form – each visitor
    the bearer of both witness and eulogy.

Life quiets, settles into the fabric of the room,
as if each breath might disturb the frailty
of remembrance. What trails we leave,
fading footprints to the past, hold tight
to the thin threads of connection:
    each ending a return, a closure, complete.

Forsaken Hymn no. 17

Each leaf a tome, unfurling: whispers of
the deeper dark, photosynthesis: the light
  absorbed, transformed into the sustenance
of thought: how each green blade bends in its wind,
not breaking, learning instead how to dance
with the gusts that guide its weaving path.

The owl's call, carried crisp through twilight's veil,
maintains the correspondence of the lost,
  a beacon in the dense, encroaching shade.
What is this constant cycle but a clock,
small hands ticking, sweeping, relentless arc
  through the silence of interwoven lives?

Below my feet, roots thread through soil: such strength
in the quiet bind, the patient grasp
that murmurs: all is connected, none alone
  in this dance of decay and renewal.
  And in this closing loop of leaf to earth,
we find our own echo, a perfect end.

Forsaken Hymn no. 18

Across the boundary where water meets the sky,
   reflections joust with the light of a sinking sun:
   ephemeral yet eternal,
   like memories of voices, carried across the waves
   from shores where no footprints remain—
haunting the twilight, science and longing entwined.

   Our thoughts spiral like the DNA's secret coil,
     linking us to every breath the forest exhales,
the symmetry in a leaf's vein, a river's meander,
    coded in the precise language of existence:
how energy transforms, how matter shifts—
nothing lost yet nothing to remain the same.

In the synthesis of this moment,
   where past whispers to future,
    I find a rooted clarity: life's persistent pulse,
our shared chapter in the vast epic
   of rising and falling tides.
   Here I stand, my soul aligned with the horizon.

Forsaken Hymn no. 19

In the afterglow's mute expanse,
I sense the delta of night's last breath:
the cool sweep of its darkening,
its shift and swirl around my stance.
    The universe: a petri dish,
expanding beneath microscope's keen eye,
we, small figments caught on the glass,

struggle, meld: our brief histories clash,
intertwining in a dance of chance
fed by starlight and the bleak silence of space.
Each moment's grain, sifted through time's wide sieve,
leaves traces: atoms dancing on the edge
of becoming or ceasing to be;
    we stand on precipices, old as earth,

our echoes cast long shadows
over mountains we cannot see,
yet feel in the throb of blood, the pulse
of heartbeats syncing with the moon's tug.
    Reflections fathom deep, stretch out
    across the void, reaching for the familiar,
    for truths woven through the fabric of days:

Forsaken Hymn no. 20

In the stillness, my heart's pulse echoes:
the subtle tug of life's intricate threads,
where roots burrow deep, yet stretch upwards,
towards the faint glow of redemption's promise.
The fabric of days: woven tight, frayed edges,
    a landscape dotted by the scars of time;
each mark a story, a lesson etched,
under the watchful gaze of a patient moon.

The current flows, a narrative unwinding,
life's river charts a course through stony grief,
bearing sediment that whispers of change:
each grain a testament to the power of flow.
Beneath the surface, turmoil and tranquility
    dance in delicate balance, crafting futures

    unseen, as water shapes stone:
    slow, relentless, a silent transformation.
Yet, amid these oscillations, clarity emerges,
    the quiet murmur grows into a song,
and I, listening deeply, find a melody
    in the convergence of past and possibility.

Forsaken Hymn no. 21

In silent halls where whispers float,
ghosts of words: past conversations,
  memories caught in cobwebbed thoughts,
tumbling through the corridors of time:
echoes not of presence but absence,
the spaces where voices used to fill.
Between pulse and silence, life quivers,

its thin thread weaving through the still:
molecular, the atoms buzz quietly,
  a slow dance of ever-shifting form,
from the warm clasp of hand to hand,
    to the cool pause between each breath,
each moment decaying, yet renewing,
its authenticity shaped by impermanence.

So, what of this thin veil, this draped curtain
    that shivers between now and thereafter?
A call, a murmur, "O come on down,"
not to darkness but deeper understanding,
where every end circles to beginnings,
and in those depths, a quiet assurance.

Forsaken Hymn no. 22

Mist floats through the morning chill:
gray tendrils over the slumbering hill,
each dewdrop a miniature echo,
   crystallizing whispers of old discords:
   how history breathes through the leaves,
fills the lungs of the land with stories.

And as the sun climbs, so does knowledge,
piercing the fog: illumination grows
in the clarity of its high noon glare.
Photosynthesizing, the green veins drink deeply,
   drawing from the soil the nectar
      of forgotten battles, silent sacrifices.

By twilight, the shadows lengthen
to curl around my thoughts:
darkness stitches the corners of what we know,
blurring the bounds of yesterday and today.
   As the last light crests the horizon,
there emerges a shared breath, closing the day.

Forsaken Hymn no. 23

Beneath the sweep of history's arc,
the fractures of our age weigh heavy:
a leaf, veins traced delicately,
    each line a path of power, stilled
by the silence that speaks in pauses:
strategic, the grin that held a world.

Here, in the quiet rustle of aged pages,
echoes stir: they are thunder, distant,
yet insistent, mapping the dance
of brilliance teetering on the brink
of oblivion, each choice a ripple
across time's vast, unseen shores.

What shadows linger in the folds
of legacy, where triumphs nestle
    close to failures, stones in streams?
My thoughts wander, bridges built
    over gaps of understanding, reaching
for closure in the cycle of stars.

Forsaken Hymn no. 24

As dawn pulls the night's blanket away:
the crows debate in raucous cries,
my voice a thread spun across the sky,
looping through the wet thick air:
each word, a drop in the river's vast account.
    The sun, a diligent scholar, climbs,
notes shimmering on each ripple,
The saddhu's eyes pierce the morning guise:

meditation deep as waters, reaching
where words falter, sink beneath
the surface tension of mere speech.
Here, I stand—speaker, listener, warring yet at peace,
    monsoon songs wash over me: resonance
in each drop, verses linked like chainmail.
Crow's call, a stanza breaks, again,

as new light frays the horizon's hem:
all endings are, indeed, beginnings anew.
In the deep hues of dawn, I stand:
listening to the crows,
their cries slicing through
the thick fog, a natural discord
    aligned with the arteries of the air:

Forsaken Hymn no. 25

In the twilight of memory's stretch,
paths where light dims: my own myths
loom, long and thin, akin to the evening's
final reach beyond the grasping dusk.
  These tales, woven tightly around
the marrow of what I once knew,
    bind me, spectral loops of narrative
that both guard and confine.

Each word a breath, every silence
a count in the rhythm of living.
Across the flattened moonscape of recall,
a horizon bends: the heart's geology,
shaped by repetitive tides of thought.
  Here, my stories sediment, layer upon
layer: impressions that fossilize under

  the weight of years.
  Beneath such pressure, diamonds form,
    memories crystallize: clear,
sharp, and unyielding. Yet, the softer
    silt shifts, allowing new streams
to erode old banks, to carve
fresh courses through stubborn past.

Forsaken Hymn no. 26

Sunlight fractures through the canopy:
this mesh of leaves and light
    that patterns the forest floor
in a mosaic of time and shadow:
each leaf a miniature sundial,
    marking hours never wholly the same.

Below, the cycle of decay and growth—
mold and mushroom at their feast:
Nature's quiet reclaimers at work,
unhurried by the tick of human clocks,
    sustained by the ceaseless chore of breaking
down what once lived to feed what lives.

    Yet, here, in this continuum, a pause—
a breath where the heart syncs with the subtle,
    and all human pursuits seem transient as mist:
how easily we dissolve into the grander narrative,
      woven into the endless fabric of being,
finding in our endings the seeds of beginning anew.

Forsaken Hymn no. 27

In the lush spread of the James River,
green unfolds: life breathes, burgeons,
   wild with the pulse of the primordial;
here, the heart hangs, feather-light,
between myth and the concrete,
where Archie finds solace in tales.

Flight casts shadows over vibrant greens,
   inner grayness wrestling with sky's expanse:
   the stability of the steady plane, a contrast
to the restless migrant heart below;
   pleas to spirits unseen, voices of ancient earth,
seeking shelter in the arms of the wild.

Thoughts drift, caught in the dance of leaves,
      pondering our deep, often silent yearnings;
how we shake the brightest sun from darker days,
   not just surviving the chill but thriving;
in the soft, green whispers of renewal,
Spring returns, urging harmony with life's song.

Forsaken Hymn no. 28

Along the snow's edge, where white eats shadows:
  it is here my thoughts unravel,
    the world, a loom of ice and sharp light:
yet beneath, life in hibernation waits,
  dreaming of its own thaw,
potent with held breath.

This landscape recalls the barker's echoes:
past harmonies felt, not seen,
each note a pulse in the white vastness—
how absence shapes our mourning,
a contour map of unseen footprints,
the chill pressing inward.

Crystals glitter, indifferent to my witness,
    yet I stand, they shine: interlocked in gaze,
the cycle of freeze and melt,
endlessly echoing a world in flux:
    ice sculptures of time, melting,
yet by melting, they shape anew.

Forsaken Hymn no. 29

In this place: a confluence where lost
memories drift, like fallen petals caught
on a stream's cool back, slipping past:
each moment's weight, more profound
than its physicality: these echoes that bind
us to what we loved, to what we must release.

    The sweep of time carves deep, unseen
channels in our minds, flowing with
the unsubstantial silts of the past:
  a geography marked by absence,
its contours shaded in the hues
of nostalgia, sharp as a winter dawn.

    Yet, in the quiet stir of morning,
where light breaks through the thin
  frost of forgetfulness, I find
a stillness ripe with potential:
    here, amid the specters of old grief,
  there is room enough to breathe anew.

Forsaken Hymn no. 30

noted simply as another layer: one
of countless others, folded into
   the strata of shared stories:
each layer, a whisper, a wound healed by time:
the soil's embrace tells of cycles:
rebirths, erosions, all cast in dust's archive:
such is the power of a simple plot:

land where seeds of the past germinate:
thinking of Archie, his hands deep in the past,
unearthing fragments that speak louder
than the cacophony of the ever spinning now:
how he found narrative in bone and shard:
   so, too, my pen digs, though not in earth:
sculpting silence into speech,

transforming the void into form:
  here, in the spaces between words,
   lies the labor of connecting:
our stories, pieced together, form the whole.
Where once I might have grasped
a shovel, now I wield syntax and sentiment.

Forsaken Hymn no. 31

mere thoughts scatter like seeds on the wind:
how we map the constellations in our minds,
each star a pinprick in the vast fabric: the universe,
    not just overhead but woven within our very cells,
connecting us to distant galaxies and the neighbor's
garden where tomatoes ripen in the soft clutch of sun.

We trace the arc of a bird's flight, think of orbits,
    celestial and simple: the round paths apples take
falling, always, toward the core of everything.
    The gravity of being pulls us into its embrace—
    a reminder: we are not loose threads but part
of a tapestry, threaded through the eye of existence.

In this room, with the gentle strum of a guitar,
echoes build bridges across the silence—
a chord that vibrates in the chest, resonates
with the unsaid words of the heart.
    Herein lies the symphony of simple things,
    connecting the pulse of life to the final note of day.

Forsaken Hymn no. 32

Leaves whisper the decay of summer:
  how light, bending through branches,
    flickers—a Morse of sorts—in the cooling air;
cycles reveal their design: repetitive,
  yet never quite the same in the details
    of leaf-vein or the speckled back of beetles.

In the quiet mathematics of existence,
  equations of sunlight parse through
the canopy: photosynthesis, the lush,
green energy converting brightness
    into life, an organic transmutation
    woven deeply into the fabric of the forest.

Roots, tangled as thoughts, penetrate
the rich, dark loam: seeking, absorbing,
mysterious in their silent, vital quest.
  And I, observer, caught in the web of it,
find each breath a testament to interconnection:
a world continuous, whole, and ever unbowed.

Forsaken Hymn no. 33

In my hand, the apple's cold weight:
an echo of that banquet hall,
a sphere spinning through dimness,
pausing time, a breath held in flight.
Air thick as history in this quiet study,
whispers of Alexander: god, man, ruler, friend.
Each choice a sharp edge slicing

what once was united—no simple rift.
The gravity in pauses, in the silence
between sword and surrender: our own
    daily battles, the turn of an apple
   in flight: a drift towards chaos or control.
Power and peril balanced in a palm,
   the potential to heal or harm

   in the whisper of a leaf's descent
or the storm contained in a simple seed.
How thin the thread that holds us
together, yet how strong it appears
in the quiet aftermath, as I ponder
the weight of a moment, decisions
made in the weightless space between.

Forsaken Hymn no. 34

In the dim dawn light, scattered sounds
echo, a shotgun's distant thunder:
like a drumbeat, firm, almost primal,
rising from Earth's deep-chested cavity.
How it mirrors the human pulse:
rapid, in the throes of action.

Each shot: a word in the vocabulary
of betrayal, the language of survival,
twisting through trees, a sinew-snapped
warning, or is it just a man asserting
his place in the wild? Skeins of smoke
blend with mist, a curtain drawn on certainty.

He might ponder, between breaths,
the schism of sky and leaf, the seamless
meld that divides and joins his world:
how one pulls the trigger and in that split
instant, nature recoils, shivers, as if
knowing: all ends are merely beginnings anew.

Forsaken Hymn no. 35

In the cool thrum of intellectual ferment,
    festive air cradles murmurs of thought:
each whisper: a peel of silvery laughter,
    each laugh: a link in the long chain of seeking.
Around me, minds converge in quickened step,
a gavotte around the ghost of my sister, Marylou.

Bright banners of dialogue wave in lofty halls,
    knowledge—the thread through narrow needle eyes,
as pages turn, tenure dances its fleeting jig.
    Seasons shift inside these venerable walls:
    yet the core remains, unyielding, driven—
    a constant hunt for truths unseen, unspent.

How the mind twirls, a dervish in quiet revelry,
through transient roles of leader, learner—both fickle.
Underneath, a steadfast pulse of inquiry,
a seeking past the tangible, into the spirit's weave.
In this arena of perpetual quest, I find solace:
the dance eternal, always beginning, never complete.

Forsaken Hymn no. 36

In the sweep of vast cosmos, molecules dance:
stars birth and die in such cold expanse.
Beneath, I tread on fallen dreams,
where light once fled from astral seams.
Change traces its arc like a comet's tail—
the inevitable course that grand scales entail.
Here, the echoes of high ambition,

reduce to whispers, a soft admission.
Energy shifts from phase to phase:
destruction, creation—a binding maze.
The entropic silence is not devoid
  of the murmur, the faint voices enjoyed.
  The cycle turns: decay becomes seed,
each ending a start, following need.

In this rotation, observed from the ground,
I find the unity in all things bound.
Seasons mirror this grand parade,
    life to death, in light and shade.
A leaf once green, now amber, falls,
settles to earth—it quietly calls.

Forsaken Hymn no. 37

We are like the weather, shifting:
daily rifts and dances, sun one minute,
   storm clouds gathering the next: life,
  a flux of light and shadow: a play
where characters evolve, revealing
complexities not easily defined.

In the lingering presence of the Old Gentleman,
I see nature's paradox: his eyes old as hills,
gleaming with youthful tricks, and his laugh,
that hints at thunder rumbling softly under calm skies:
he speaks in breezes, whispers and gales,
touching the soul softly or tearing it wide.

He leaves impressions like footprints in wet earth,
   soon washed away by rain or blown into new patterns
    by indifferent winds: we are all so temporary,
yet rooted deeply in each experience.
  And when he finally departs, leaving silence,
it resonates like a stone settled at the bottom of a lake.

Forsaken Hymn no. 38

The leaves whisper down: their crisp:
  voices: patterns of descent
calculated by the tilt
 of the earth, the pull, minute and exact,
   of moon's shy persuasion:
our friends fall, silent in their drift.

Each name, a leaf once green, now bright
or dulled by the sun's long kiss:
soil's claim, its immutable embrace:
Old friends—
their stories feed roots, grow the future
  from remnants of the past.

  In the quiet, I hear the hush, feel
the cycle: the meeting, the parting,
the layers of loss and gain:
   truths, like Horace's old shadows,
   seek light, intricate and subtle,
    and in this slow dance, find peace.

Forsaken Hymn no. 39

In twilight's soft whisper: a science:
atoms dance, unseen, yet felt
in the chill that climbs the evening air,
    structuring the fading light into coolness:
the daily resignation of warmth:
  a meticulous transition we barely sense:

Here, through the heart's microscope,
we observe our own vast spaces
as shadows lengthen, pulling taut
    their delicate threads: the connections
that twine through our existence,
  binding us to dusk's inevitable arrival:

Leaves rustle, a murmur of continuity:
the constant composition of beginnings,
    woven into ends: thus, we traverse
each moment: a path laid in contrasts,
  our steps echoing between what was,
the patterns unfolding into what must be.

Forsaken Hymn no. 40

In this garden where I rake and contemplate,
each leaf: a memory or a lost dream,
down to the molecular whispers of decay:
here, where roots intertwine with my own,
growth and rot marking the same passage,
in the cool, damp cradle of earth's embrace.

Leaves rustle—a discourse on transience—
    and the sky, infinite, mirrors my thoughts,
clouds sauntering across: a slow, gray waltz,
while I stand, a figure hemmed by horizons,
each breath a frontier between now and then,
all the while shadows stretch, reaching out.

The day closes, colors bleeding into dusk,
each moment distilled into hues of solitude,
and here, amidst the quiet descent into night,
I gather scattered pieces, a mosaic of self,
whispers of my sister's laughter in the wind,
    a final leaf falls, and I, too, find ground.

Forsaken Hymn no. 41

The woods stretch out: each tree a witness,
roots deep in the frost-hardened soil: they
    hold secrets beneath the ice-crusted surface,
      whispers of those who walked before—
the crunch of their steps a quiet testament
to cycles of life, death, rebirth.

Amidst the brittle branches, the sky
bleeds the last light of day:
nature's slow exhale into twilight,
while a hawk circles, precise and patient,
its keen eyes charting the murmur
of the earth: each movement its map.

And here I stand, interwoven:
listening as the dusk deepens,
    the shadows merge—death is not
an end but a transformation:
      we are, each of us, entwined in this
    vast, endless cycle of becoming.

Forsaken Hymn no. 42

The echo of my step in the corridor
of the mind: a slow patter, soft and unsure,
marks time like a pulse beneath the hard shell
of the cosmos, this too is a type of journey:
where thought spirals into deep celestial bodies,
matter dense with the atoms of ancients.

   The inheritance of madness, a lineage
woven through the DNA spirals,
a chromosome's dusty path: I trace
   the origins of wandering minds, scattered
   like pollen on the winds of harsh survival,
   each gust a question in silence: where next?

In the quiet, I sift through the rubble
of battles lost and won within,
   and the peace sought like distant thunder,
   soft and rumbling, promising renewal.
   Here, in the stillness after storms,
   I find the quiet end of asking.

Forsaken Hymn no. 43

Roots twist into the dense earth:
each a question curled in darkness,
feeding from microscopic exchanges:
   nutrients for a hint of sunbeam.
The oak branches: fractals against the blue,
mimic the lungs' delicate pathways:
how air flows, fills, sustains:

how leaf breathes and branch sways.
   Underneath: the unseen work of worms,
silent, shifting, enriching soil:
turning decay to dark, fertile promise:
   life from lifelessness: a slow alchemy.
Sunset's photons cast long shadows,
threads of light weave through leaves:

a tapestry in green and gold,
each thread a pulse in the vast web.
The cool air whispers of coming night,
   dew gathers like thoughts on grass:
how simple, this cycle of breath,
of day into night: of growth, of rest.

Forsaken Hymn no. 44

In twilight's hush, a smoldering whisper:
nature's own voice crackles, a dialect
   only fire-scorched leaves and brittle bark
seem to comprehend: here lies truth, tangled
in the ashes, and above, the moon observes,
      its cool glow a stark contrast to the blaze.

Flames dance fiercely with the night,
each leap a story of ruin and rebirth:
how easily the strong succumb,
   how quietly the weak endure, scattered
      like seeds on the breath of chaos,
awaiting rain to quench their thirst.

      Amid the dance, a deeper silence calls,
echoing across the canopy: the promise
of renewal in the heart of destruction,
winds shift, carrying cool whispers—
      hope cradled in the arms of storms,
and at last, peace descends, complete.

Forsaken Hymn no. 45

In chambers of shadow and echo, I roam:
walls lean close, whisper of decay and dawn,
each crack a testament to time's relentless chisel.
Memory's corridors, lined with ghosts
of past missteps—how they grasp
   at the frayed edges of now.

I once danced here with ruin, intimate
and estranged: her grip cold, her gaze
  indifferent, as if our past was a tale
told by someone else.
  Time spins, and partners change,
rhythm lost in the shift of shadows.

Now, in the ruins' reflective eye,
  I search for old rhythms, find
only a stranger's calm betrayal.
   Ruin, no longer familiar, mirrors
not the past, but the passage:
every end, a new beginning.

Forsaken Hymn no. 46

whispered secret seems:
   a sudden silence, a small universe
     expanding between the seams of noise:
here, the lining of a cloud, silver and withdrawn,
   echoes the hidden paths water takes,
     sculpting canyons in its wake.

   The sirens bleed into birdcalls
as dawn mutates the sky:
transmutation, not of alchemy,
   but of the purest form of physics,
     where light divides and scatters,
forming spectra not meant to last.

Yet, in this ephemeral play of colors,
each shade persists longer than a glance,
   like the varied tones of leaves before the fall,
dancing to the ground, each descent
a whispered end, a cycle spun anew:
so every ending crafts its beginning.

Forsaken Hymn no. 47

In the early light, molecules dance:
air, an unseen choreographer,
guides pollen in balletic drift—
how particles traverse not just space
but the quiet moments between,
the breath where thought pivots:

And I: how much space do I cross daily,
not the span, but the depth?
   Every step into the grass whispers
histories, the weight of dew heavy
   like memories upon each blade,
maintenance of the fragile dance:

We are not disparate from these cycles,
atoms bound in a broader choreography,
each one of us caught in the pull
and sway of cosmic rhythms.
My footsteps map the route,
but my presence spans infinity: closure.

Forsaken Hymn no. 48

Silence follows the shout: we stand,
the ripples of foreign syllables
   dissolving into air: how strange
the sound of another's heritage breaking
    like waves upon the shores of our understanding.
Our worlds overlap in thin, trembling circles:
I recall the entropy of closed systems,

the order that arises spontaneously,
how energy scatters, spreads out,
seeking to fill every hollow with a whisper.
   No words can hold the full weight
of reality: every language stumbles,
short of the eternal, grappling with
the transient patterns of existence:

All is transient but the transformation.
The skin of the apple browns:
exposure to air, to the invisible rush
of time and oxygen, an oxidation,
a quiet fire that consumes the fresh
flesh turning it, slowly, irreversibly.

Forsaken Hymn no. 49

In this dimming, the cat finds corners:
    not for fear, but for the textured shadows
that speak: low, the kind of murmur that slips
from light to twilight, telling of time
compressed, each moment feathered, fleeting—
    like sand through fingers, it falls, whispering
its soft descent: can we grasp the grains,

or do they, too, dream of escape, leaving
only the warmth of their passing touch
as hints of presence, of what was once held—
    so the cat dreams, whiskers twitch: a twitch
spurred by the chase of days he can't recall:
    and I listen for the pulse of his breath,
    steady yet waning, a rhythm syncing

    with the slow dance of decline: knowing
    our own furrows deepen in the dance.
    Even the moon seems muted tonight, casting
    a pallid light that sketches faint outlines
on the earth: a fragile old cat, edges
blurring into the shadows of decline.

Forsaken Hymn no. 50

In the vast silence, space begins:
   its endless dance of cold light and darker patches,
each movement a silent note
    in the cosmic score: here I listen—
the thrum of heart against the void,
   sparks of existence humming softly.

War tools lie cold in hand: steel
meets skin, yet feels nothing—
    unlike the stars, who know when to blink out,
or the blues, weaving through the gloom,
a rhythm: pulsing, alive,
opposed to the still sterility of my grip.

Outside, infinity stretches, pulling
the soul toward both light and shadow:
    in this fabric, threads of war weave with whispers
of peace, the tender shoots beneath hard frost.
    So, do I forge or break, creator or destroyer?
These questions linger, resolved as I stand, a sentinel caught.

Forsaken Hymn no. 51

The sea whispers: continuity,
rolling its depths to the brim
of the shore: the same ancient
beat: molecular, vast, as cold
as the void between stars, where
time stretches, indifferent to loss.

Stars glisten like ice in veins
of dark matter: how strangely
they bind us: illumination
born from ignition, their slow
exhaustion a mirror to our
small, burning lives.

We reach toward that endless pulse,
our hands churning histories in
the sands: ephemeral yet full
of the night's cold truths. Each wave
retracts, a breath returning to the source,
leaving us quiet, at last, on the shore.

Forsaken Hymn no. 52

Amid the disarray, a hard new angle:
the vise grips the pine-scented air,
its steel jaws the cold harbinger
   of change: once tools laid ready, now
silent besides this stoic intruder,
antithesis of the crafted wood's warm grain.

Embracing shadows, a workshop unfamiliar,
   wrestles with my tranquility,
a split notion: obstruction, or
    opportunity to mold unknown alloys
of thought, the fusion of iron's chill
   with the tender curvatures of heartwood.

Could this be the pivot, a swing
   to unforeseen architectures? Yes,
each spanner and chisel
   reintroduced, every sweep of sawdust
   a scripture of adaptation,
    the vise, after all, a teacher in resilience.

Forsaken Hymn no. 53

In the quiet chaos that blankets the earth,
my back pressed into forgiving dirt,
    I hear whispers: Hardy, Housman,
    choosing silence over clamor:
     their quietude, a refuge,
as leaves rustle their assent.
    Above, the sky stretches, vast and complex,
a mirror to my teeming thoughts:

    its simple blue, an infinite mystery—
    both shield and invitation.
Kierkegaard's yearnings echo here,
desiring blindness to relentless news.
    Surrounded by the hum of life unchanged,
    reflecting on the skin we wear as walls,
our structures frail yet persistently enveloped,
  in the sounds of earth's deep breaths,

the sky's profound expanse above:
a disquieting peace settles within.
Amid our entangled existences,
    our shared dance with impending oblivion,
    pondering the weight of human tapestries—
are we caught in nets from which we strive
to escape, or weaving connections
  that hold more than they confine?

Forsaken Hymn no. 54

Each round cycles like seasons:
the cold touch of winter in sterile light,
shadows stretch, curl at the edges
of my confined life, seeking space
beyond a sign, starkly hung: NO VISITORS—
a barrier as real as any wall.

My heart gathers the images of faces,
memories flickering like flames on a string:
An old girlfriend and a woman in Seattle—
parts of a whole in the flash of their eyes,
guardrails on my weakening frame,
   mocking the walk I once mastered.

Echoes of laughter, once loud in the halls,
   now whispers under the hum of machines.
   My breath follows the rhythm of drips,
luminous syringes singing clarity
      into veins, mapping the final connections
of a life, ending but whole at last.

Forsaken Hymn no. 55

In the silence of narrow spaces,
the geometry of a room: calculated,
sharp angles where shadows fold
   into themselves: dark origami of thought.
  Our dialogue: a delicate dance
of evasion, a play of light and absence,
where words, like moths, flutter
against the quiet, seeking a breach

in the cocoon of our making,
each flutter a subtle betrayal.
  She shifts, and the air tenses,
as if the room exhales its chill—
betraying us both, its frost a mirror
to our frost-bound exchange.
A martini's clear ice reflects
more than light: truths unspoken,

flickers of regret, the cold edge of glass
   that cuts deeper than speech:
   bold in its silence, profound
in its containment. We sit,
  the space between us drawing
  tight as a bowstring poised
with questions left hanging,
   arrows unaimed but ready.

Forsaken Hymn no. 56

In twilight's calm expanse: I muse,
how nature's script, unmarred by flame,
writes in the ashes left by fire,
　　the renewal sewn in silt and seed.
Our world, draped in quiet, does not
cease; it breathes through scattered ruins,
　　and in the microscopic dance

of atoms, finds paths to persist.
Growth from decay, an endless loop:
the core of all our living tales,
　　each moment's cease a start anew,
and every end a thread to weave.
　　The seer's crystal, dreaming still
of mundane fates, forgets: the vast

array of stars are born from dust,
condensed in silent, brilliant birth.
Where death appears to claim its due,
life's pulse throbs on, in unseen depths;
　　every cessation is a cloak
for genesis beneath the folds.

Forsaken Hymn no. 57

The juice clings: the sharp, sweet tang, a reminder
of days when sun spilled over us, unfiltered
and fierce: does the heart know what the tongue tastes
or does it remember the pulse, the running wild?
Such thoughts tumble with the rustle of fallen leaves,
the crunch underfoot a dialogue between now
and then: the soil receives all confessions,
  disposing them through endless cycles of rebirth.

Breath quivers in the chill: a shiver, a ghost
  of adrenaline, fragrant with youth's reckless spice;
it lingers as if to argue that even the calm
and the collected have chaos beneath,
  waiting, like seeds, for the storm to release them.
Time's passage echoes in the hush between light
and darkness: a star's flicker, a bat's wingbeat,

  both fleeting yet imprinted in the mind's vast sky;
how we seek and flounder in the night's tender fold.
  Nature, the great mirror, reflects back our days,
smooths the rough edges of our laughter and cries;
each setting sun, like a folded letter, seals
yet another chapter, a story told in whispers
that the wind carries away, over top of trees,
  into the boundless reverie of the stars.

Forsaken Hymn no. 58

Amidst the flow of time and thought,
my mind's eye sees: strands tightly drawn,
across wide fields of what we ought,
   and what we lose: the dusk, the dawn.
     The constants, like the sun that sets,
initiate the nightly fears:
what mattered once, in silhouettes,

embraces shadows, disappears.
Yet, in this dance of light and dark,
the cycle turns: the seasons show
   how bonds may bend, may leave a mark,
or fade, the way warm breezes go.
     Through nature, life's relentless pulse,
a heart's echo, a whisper's weight,

   finds balance in the grand repulse
of ending as it began, sedate.
     The paths we tread weave deep, then part:
our shared moments, the stars' brief light,
each step a beat of the vast heart,
closing gentle, into the night.

Forsaken Hymn no. 59

In the chime of a bell, a question is called:
  how does the past shape the labyrinth of now?
 Its echo, a shadow cast deep and vague,
melds with the cobblestone underfoot: each a relic,
each a whisper in the continuity of rust and resolve.
  Time spirals, as ivy climbing the old stone walls:
persistent, invasive, enshrining what once was
  with the verdant vigor of what could be:

is this not the dance of decay and growth?
Death, life intertwined in the roots of existence,
    breathing through the same stem of necessity.
And here we stand: anointed not just by history,
but by the very act of remembering,
  cherishing not just the grandeur, but
    the fall, the rise, the humbled knees—
for every end cradles the fragile breath of beginnings,

closing not in silence, but an invitation to witness.
In the weave of cool stone: each arch,
a testament to ascent and collapse, stone
that has seen empires rise and weather
into whispers: how lightly lies the dust
of the powerful, the cries of bells spill,
echoing over cobbles, around, through.

Forsaken Hymn no. 60

In the whispering twilight, hues blend:
 day into night, man into mankind,
each boundary a faint line in the sand,
eroded by the gentle tides of time:
still, a whisper, icy and persistent,
murmurs of lines not yet dissolved.
  Beneath the surface, the sediment
of old biases clings tight to the roots,

deep and unseen, like the dark
matter that binds galaxies:
 Here, in the shadows, Archie speaks
of walls invisible but impermeable.
In the shared flight, pilots navigate
the same storm-laden skies,
the spinning world beneath, impartial,
observes not the color but the craft.

The pinkie without a hand reminds us:
we are incomplete, interconnected.
  Archie, spectral in the gloaming,
   echoes, "Most peoples gonna lose,"
and in this common loss, maybe,
we find the threads of unity,
  the necessity of each, the whole.

Forsaken Hymn no. 61

"Trust your comrades," seems an almost
sacred vow, made beneath this immutable sphere:
a bond sealed in the brevity of a heartbeat,
    and as lasting as the craters that scar
  its cold, ancient face.
The trees here whisper of continuity:
their roots, intertwined, delve deep into histories

    not written but rather absorbed,
water and nutrient mixed with the essence
of countless valiant departures,
each leaf a stanza in the lore of survival.
    Beyond, the grasses sway with the grace
of unspoken secrets, the gentle rustle

a language of persistence: resilience
    encoded in every bend and recovery.
  Streams, too, carry the burden of remembrance,
their fluid stories coursing through veins
of the land, murmuring: we endure—
and in enduring, remember all.

Forsaken Hymn no. 62

In the hedge's shadow, the rabbit hides:
    each twitch, a calculated whisper:
how closely life clings to the quick edge
   of survival, the delicate balance
between seen and unseen, known and unknown:
every moment, a leaf flutter away.

The garden knows this dance well, its soil
rich with the decay of yesterday,
feeding today: life cycles, unbroken,
    in which death burgeons, sprouts into the new,
roots intertwining like thoughts, reaching deep,
beneath what is visible, felt in the dark.

So, too, my thoughts cycle back to nature,
    each pondering root wrapped around earth's truths:
we, beings of both shadow and light,
navigate through seasons of the self,
  finding in each careful step, a path:
a way home through the intricate wild.

Forsaken Hymn no. 63

In the dim echo of twilight, I ponder
the existence of bats, unburdened by our ties:
no bankers to heed, no taxes to pay, no
   arrests darkening their dusk flights: thus, they spin
through the dark, wings cut from the cloth of night,
driven by instinct and sharp echolocation.

Confined within walls lined with dusty books,
   I sit under the hum of electric thoughts,
reflecting on Archie's flight from our world,
yearning, perhaps, for the simplicity
   and the freedom nestled in the cave's cold heart.
His cousins know this refuge well: shadows' grace.

How often we, draped in civilization's fabric,
   dream of such unencumbered existence.
The bats, with their radar, flit crisis-free
through cool air, while I remain entangled in
knowledge's duty, eyes gleaming with false light.
   Saluting the cave's solace over glare's bind.

Forsaken Hymn no. 64

The leaf's edge: crisp, fractal, precise—
    its contours a map of the whispering wind,
leading thoughts to the greater circuit:
how energy flows from sun to sinew.
Atoms dance in the marrow of the world,
    binding and breaking: the alchemy of life.
Beneath our feet, roots tangle with buried cables,

a symphony of organic and the wrought—
    each thriving on currents, unseen yet felt:
the pulse of the earth, the buzz of human hubris.
    Night's coolness pulls dew from the breath of soil,
painting each blade of grass with a universe:
small, reflective worlds, fleeting as thought.
    The stars wheel overhead, indifferent to our scurry,

    connected by the very forces that shove us apart.
Do we not, too, orbit something unseen?
Binary systems: push and pull, in and out,
a celestial dance of balance and tumult.
Does the tree lament its autumn loss, or
embrace the nakedness of its truth?

Forsaken Hymn no. 65

Under the vaulting sky: a freshness
that speaks to the green sapling in me,
longing—: for sunlight: for rain.
This is the journey of water:
  from cloud to stream, seeping
into the earth: the roots waiting.
Each leaf unfurls, a testament

to the cycles: the boundless dance:
sun coaxing chlorophyll: life.
I ponder the delicate balance,
    the ebb and flow of days,
each carrying its portion of shadow.

How like the moon, my heart
    waxes and wanes: a reflection
in a pool of still water, deep.
The crickets sing their truth—
that all life stirs with the same breath:
the cosmos whirring softly.

Forsaken Hymn no. 66

Amid the lush palms where shadows play,
the silent monk confronts the blaze:
his peace, a stark, unyielding light
against the dark antics of power's maze.
The world spins, relentless, framed
by such contrasts: fire and calm,
the choreography of leaves in wind,

each gesture a world, poised, yet embalmed.
In the spinning globe of green and gray,
   I see the politician, nimble, a reed in storm,
his laughter rings, devoid of weight,
floating above the moral norm.
But underneath, the tremor of doubt,
of souls wrestling with the fabric torn:

   is this the weave of all our days,
      this patchwork of the forlorn?
   The scene folds into the valleys of my mind,
      whispering through the canyon of my thoughts:
in nature's inexorable script, I read
a lesson the fluttering shadow taught.

Forsaken Hymn no. 67

In the balance of breath and blade,
each slice: a delicate inquiry—
    how life hangs, filament fine,
  on decisions made beneath the skin.
The scalpel traces not just tissue
but the borders of my own resolve.

Light dims: a challenge casts its cold
    on my hands, agents of healing,
      or agents of harm, questioning
    which will they manifest today?
Silence speaks in pressures, pulses,
blood's rhythm, slow, then swift.

Into myself I delve, seeking
within the dark for that spark
that animates the soul's soft machinery—
hands moving with practiced poise,
repairing what is torn, soothing
what is frayed, till all is stitched whole.

Forsaken Hymn no. 68

I wandered through the echoes of a jazz-filled night,
  the air vibrant with the soulful cry of a saxophone:
    a universe expanded in a melody, swirling—
particles of sound like dust motes in sunlight,
where physics meets the feral beat of human hearts:
each note a microcosm, vibrating, infinite.

Vibration: a bridge between the seen and unseen,
notes cascading like a river over pebbles,
each stone shaped by the water's tireless tongue:
the patterned randomness, the chaos ordered by flow,
    and I, standing amidst the fluid dynamics,
      ponder the forces sculpting soul and stone alike.

So what binds us, here, under the cosmic swing,
    but invisible threads pulled by gravity's soft fingertips?
Each life, each atom drawn in rhythmic dance,
  circling back to the night's deep pulse,
    where all ends and begins in breathless sync—
thus, in the silence after, we hear the whole song.

Forsaken Hymn no. 69

In the dimming glow of an evening squandered,
Whispers of light tease the edges of thought:
How do tendrils of affection wind so tightly,
Binding us in silent, expectant loops,
    Only to dissolve into the ether,
A vapor ungrasped by the heart's reach?

  Arcing over the void of connection,
This space between intent and reception,
He crafts orbits from his longing,
    Each path calculated in the precision
Of celestial bodies lost in space—
  Hope drifting, yet anchored in the stars.

    But what is the measure of a sigh,
Lost in the vastness of the night?
Does the universe echo the resonance
  Of desires unfulfilled, or do we cast
Alone our dreams against the vast silence,
  Only to find peace in the release?

Forsaken Hymn no. 70

As dawn breaks, the horizon sparks:
its light, a diffusion through canopy cracks,
  each beam a conductor of the day's symphony—
nature's breath in the rustle, the murmur
of leaves; roots entwining in the quiet earth,
growing unseen, yet profoundly felt.

Beneath the vast sky, I chart my course:
    meticulous as the ant that scales the pebble,
persistent as water carving its bed in stone.
This journey—layered and sedimented with time,
where moments compound: the pressure
into diamonds, the fleeting into permanence.

    And when the dusk descends, cooling the air,
the day's labor settles into the folds of the night;
my oar pauses, floating gently by the dock.
The stars: not just lights, but echoes of the cosmos,
    reminders of cycles, unending, larger than lifetimes.
In this vast web, I find my place, quietly complete.

Forsaken Hymn no. 71

Roots twist deep, where dark soils:
feed vast networks unseen,
   a silent mesh beneath the frenzied
     surface where rain sings the stone
    to smoothness, each drop
a note in the symphony of decay.

Above, the storm gathers, pulling:
  threads of cloud into dense hymns,
    nature conducting its breathless orchestra
in sweeps of wind, each gust
sculpting air, bending trees to its will,
leaves fluttering like eager hearts.

Through the tempest's veil, I see:
moments as transient as raindrops on leaves,
    each story told a ripple in the pond,
my voice a stone thrown in wide arcs,
landing in the stillness of the after-rain,
  everything settles—stories root like seeds.

Forsaken Hymn no. 72

Beneath these soaring branches, caught:
the dance of shadows, light splayed
across the face of innocence:
a child swings, each arc a story
of rise and fall, the pendulum
swaying between joy and gravity.

Amidst the rustle, statutes stand,
silent spectators cast in stone:
their eyes, unblinking, trace the bounds
of fleeting laughter and the weight
of time, worn deep into the lines
etched by history's steady hand.

And here, where leaves whisper of law,
the air thick with the musk of earth,
truths surface, tender as new shoots:
the swing slows, arcs diminish,
yet in this final, lingering sway—
all our complexities rest, resolved.

Forsaken Hymn no. 73

Between stones: the moss whispers
its slow, green growth over years
   that will outlast my footprints here,
a quiet chronicle of patience: day
merges into night: cycles seen
    only by the stillness of rock.

Each grain of sand, meticulously raked,
forms lines like ripples on a lake,
   drawn by a monk's steady hand: each wave
a breath, each breath a thought,
all converging in the garden's calm:
   this art of precision and release.

In this play of permanence and shift,
I find lessons in the layered quiet,
   in how change molds us, soft
  as moss, firm as stone,
and finally, in the settling dusk,
the garden breathes completeness.

Forsaken Hymn no. 74

The day collapses into specks of dark;
   twilight breathes a last gasp of faded gold:
nature's reliquary, where old ghosts walk
through whispered leaves, each step a story told.
Yet these do not soften the clench of grief,
a fist around the fraying threads of soul.

How the city lights mock the starry sky,
   their luminous counterfeit, weak yet bold,
pales before the vast, unyielding night:
but still, Archie's despair, too vast to hold,
   threads through the cosmos, unwound yet tight,
in the fabric where universes fold.

   Sorrow, like gravity, draws all to core,
spiraling down to the singularity:
here, amidst the grandeur and the lore,
human pain finds its own clarity.
   From whispered ache to echoing roar,
the end of each layer: sincerity.

Forsaken Hymn no. 75

    Light dives through canopies: minnows
in the vast ocean of air, stars glimpsing
    Earth's boundless choreographies:
the lilt and sway of branches,
the relentless script of time, unfolding,
nature's manuscript untouched by hands.

Particles float, aimlessly yet directed
by the subtle pulse of atmospheric tides;
each leaf, a vessel for the sun, converts
    radiance to breath—the exhales
     of forests feeding the invisible hunger
    of our own fleeting respires.

In the quiet, beneath the ancient woody sentinels,
I perceive the slow mesh of shadows—
time weaving light and dark into tapestries
    that narrate the history of growth and decay,
and at the base, where roots clasp earth,
steadily, the world finds its closure.

Forsaken Hymn no. 76

In the quietude where whispers converge:
intersections of bone and breath,
the bareness of Archie' world reflects
    the minimum universe, every atom
a microcosm of survival, of solitude;
    each fragment articulating a simpler truth.

By the shore, the sea murmurs tales of cyclic return:
continuous waves shaping the shoreline,
eroding grains, each collapse a new formation,
a dance of persistence and surrender,
echoing the silent resilience of living
    despite the inevitability of erosion.

Shared steps by the sea's edge, footprints
that speak: our path is together woven,
fading slowly into the wet sand's embrace.
Through this communion, a melody rises—
a hymn of existence, stark yet full,
completing its chorus as twilight descends.

Forsaken Hymn no. 77

As I stand in the cold light of autumn:
   the earth prepares its final bow,
leaves whispering secrets of collapse
to the barren soil: a promise
   they fulfill in their descent.
Cycles and cells in constant spinning:
the steady decay forms the cradle

of new life: each fallen leaf,
a silent testament to the perpetual
shifts: graves and cradles intertwined.
   And here, in the quiet afternoon,
   the air tastes of transition:
      Archie's weariness becomes my cloak,
dressed in the weight of shared thoughts

on the brief blaze of impermanent flames.
   I breathe, feel the slight chill,
finding peace in this timely surrender—
a leaf, a life: each radiates its last,
then joins the undistinguished earth,
returning: always returning.

Forsaken Hymn no. 78

In the dim light, Archie vanishes:
each motion less than before, more ghost
than man, and I, trailing his shrinking form,
find often, the substance of his thoughts
feeds me more than bread: his words, the seeds
from which my own tangled roots spread deep
into the dark, fertile soil of inquiry.

   He speaks in the whisper of leaves,
recites the calculus of change
with every breath, his exhale a theorem
   proved in the gradual wither of flesh.
We are ephemeral, like wisps of morning fog
lifted by the sun's relentless assay,
or rain upon the thirsty pavement:

   so brief, yet part of a larger thirst,
   a cycle that spins slow, then fast.
   Archie's life, folded into memory's archive,
warns and teaches by erosion's gentle art:
how to stand resilient as the oak,
knowing well the axe's blade sharpens
   near the heartwood, yet still, we reach for light.

Forsaken Hymn no. 79

Here among giants, old as sun:
bark whispers to root: one limb flung
across millennia, reaching for light:
why does history shade so ambiguously?
   Does the sparrow feel the weight
of its own fleeting form against the sky,
   or does it merely sweep along the currents:

   airs of lesser density: patterns seen from high?
I walk and ponder, Archie, your vastness:
a legacy, entangled like these roots,
deep in the fertile floor: a mesh
of deeds and myths, blending silently.
   The leaves rustle with the magnitude

   of your departure: the forest, undiminished,
yet acknowledges: a void where once
a mighty energy surged, touching all.
The air, thick with stories of Archie,
   drifts, permeates the very essence
of space, sculpting shadows out of sunlight:

Forsaken Hymn no. 80

Time turns in gyrations, unfixed but precise:
branches nod to the cadence of seasons,
    to the wind's sharp scythe,
    each leaf a microcosm: breathing,
        in decay finding design,
the blueprint of wither and flourish.

    In this cosmic play: my role—
bit player on the edge
of the stage, watching the sky's grand opera,
endless rewrites of cloud and clarity,
where the sun fades into a smear
of blush, the signature of day's end.

My hands, coated in the soil
    of toil, bear the stigmata of labor—
        roots, and seeds, and the hope
of growth sown deep in the earth.
This terrain, worked over, my existential plot:
a place to stand, or from which to depart.

Forsaken Hymn no. 81

through cracks in time: springs unravel threads,
leaf whispers, mud-stained chasms: how life begins
anew through blinks of dark: merging, dying:
   in seams: where mineral meets root: inflections
of earth bones, aged arboreal tales told
in the quietness of sedimentary beds:
the slow creek knows: erosion is a script,

each grain of sand a letter spelled by currents,
framing this rugged narrative of change.
—

moss clings to the reft places: insistent green,
proof of persistence: softness conquers stone,
and over stone, the moss whispers: thrive, hold on:
  antennas fined as hair detect slight shifts:

the world's pulse, the turn from drought to drink,
patterns in chaos, wind-drawn, sun-sieved.
—

from such slender, clinging life: wisdom,
  the man's voice threading through years: we survive,
like moss: by clutching at fissures, making them home.

Forsaken Hymn no. 82

In the twilight of my gratitudes, where
good nature has wilted like the last
   rose of summer, I turn, with a philosopher's
resignation, to the small, mundane acts
of survival: the tightening of a screw,
the closing of a door against the cold.

  Here, in the cozy grave of my contemplations,
I laugh, scorn more than joy in the sound,
  at the rainbow illusions of a less cynical
     youth. Am I to bow further, Father,
or stand against the pull of an earthly burial
  before my final breath breathes out?

The names of the divine echo hollow—
Jehovah, Yahweh, God—marvelous in
  their indifference, unified in their disregard
  for my plight. And yet, as I stand isolated,
pondering my last earthly abode, strangely,
I find peace in the quiet surrender to life's endgame.

Forsaken Hymn no. 83

The earth breathes beneath my feat:
   every tremor a notebook flung
across the cosmos, pinioned by time's
relentless ink, such that every fleck
of dust remembers its origin
in the heart of ancient suns.

Each keystroke: it resonates
down through the bedrock, where atoms
      dance aside for the new etching—
   rivers carve their beds anew,
      stones shift, and in this small apocalypse,
my words find their fleeting empire.

Relieved, then, from the tyranny of the seat,
   I behold the skyline: script of cloud,
draft of the drifting day—
      The lore of simple things, enveloped
in the wide arms of horizon's embrace:
   here I am scribe; here I conclude.

Forsaken Hymn no. 84

In the simmer of a sunlit wave,
the sea whispers of its own consuming:
  each current a soft cradle, then grave,
  its power masked in gentle foaming.
    Bubbles rise, burst—life's fragile sign,
the lobster's shell an armor wrought
    by nature's ancient, slow design,

a brittle safeguard, casually bought.
Does it know fear, or merely dwell
in the bland minute before the steam?
  Do we partake or merely quell
our hunger with what might have been?
Below the boiling point, the heat
  submits its will, draws forth the red

of sacrifice: the shell's defeat
forged in the silence of the dead.
Control: the grip we think we hold,
  the systems shaping with unseen hand—
like water that can soothe or scold,
  our power slips, like time's soft sand.

Forsaken Hymn no. 85

In the folds of night, echoes drift:
a symphony of cricket chirps:
cold starlight spills down, unfiltered,
 across the landscape of my solitude:
each chill, a note played on facial nerves,
the earth's breath, a quiet observer.

The relentless ticking within—
 of clocks, of heartbeats, of fleeting time—
 intertwines with the slow decay of flesh:
 life molecules breaking down, regrouping,
as if each division could forestall
 the inevitable reclamation.

Yet, in this disassembling, a map:
routes back to renewal, to communion,
where memory's warmth thins the ice—
 fingers stretched towards the glow of hearth
 as if to hold the light, to affirm
existence is more than its end.

Forsaken Hymn no. 86

The air; thick: a burden we breathe,
fog-laden with particles, tiny and vast,
each an echo of actions cast,
judged not by gods but by gravity: a force
mercifully blind, pulling even, indiscriminate
of leaf, of stone, of us.

Molecules swirl in the current,
joining, parting: an endless dance
of chance meetings,
    chemical bonds formed and broken
    as easily as promises in the dark—
a flux fixed in nature's impartial code.

    Before the solemnity of judgment,
atoms bear no malice or intent:
    simply exist, collide, react,
then evolve where conditions favor—
turning tumult into harmony,
    wherein lies the defense against chaos.

Forsaken Hymn no. 87

In the glade, light fragments: a puzzle
left unsolved, shifting with the wind's
breath, bending twig and leaf: this dance
of shadows and whispers, so like his
    elusive grace, hints at the unspoken:
how light, too, bears the weight of mystery.

  Each step on moss, each rustle, tells
of paths converged and diverged:
the sound—a leaf's slight tear as it
hits the forest floor—mirrors the soft
snap of branches in our own lives,
making space for new growth amid the old.

Here, where roots grip earth and canopy
embraces sky, I find a momentary peace:
the forest breathes a quiet lesson of continuity,
   showing us how to stand resilient, meshed
    in life's intricate weave, until the end:
hope persists, whispered in every leaf's turning.

Forsaken Hymn no. 88

In this space where silence blooms like a stern flower,
each pause a testament to what thrives unseen:
　　the slow creep of ivy up cold stone—
　nature's unfurling script—silent and precise,
holding the potent breath of decay,
the hush before speech spills over.
　　Memory: a landscape gorged with relics—
granite, combatant against the wind's erode,

stands in defiance, though beneath, sand shifts,
　endlessly: particles in dance, bitter, sweet.
Through this, the spiders weave, adept
　at crafting survival from the sparest of threads.
So, too, the mind constructs from fragments,
caught in the loom of unspoken dreams,
　a tapestry, rich and dark with yearning,
the past's texture under fingers, felt

　　as if these moments could be held,
but, like water, slipping through the grasp.
　Here, among echoes of those who sang
and left the song unfinished, I tread,
finding in each echo a vibration tuned
to the frequency of loss, a harmonious descent
into the quietus where all songs conclude—
and in their ending, find their meaning.

Forsaken Hymn no. 89

In the twilight of minds: dreams weave
    into my waking threads: a seamless blend,
the silent vows of shadows: echo, echo:
each a whisper, each a spectral bride
crossing the threshold: of my dimming sight,
their forms: dances of light: and not-light.

I stand: a groom at the verge of knowing,
in the hall of whispers: where words bind
more than flesh: essence to essence,
a ceremony not seen but deeply felt:
    each promise a link in the chain of forever,
tying me to the echo of endless murmurs.

As the space between breaths deepens,
one voice emerges: stark against the hush,
    her luminous vow: guiding me through
    the caverns of dissolution: where every
goodbye is a silent oath: sworn anew,
and I awaken: not to day, but to profound night.

Forsaken Hymn no. 90

Amid the whisper of leaves, my thoughts:
   wander, caught in the persistent web
of past laughter echoing against
the distant murk of lost time,
    where light dilates and narrows:
answering to the rhythm of the heart.

Each step unveils another layer:
soil rich with decay and new beginnings,
    roots entwined beneath the surface,
like memories within us, branching
    deep, yet unseen, the pulse of earth
resonating with our fleeting warmth.

As twilight folds sky into shadow,
I pause: considering the crimson fade—
a closure not of dark, but of light
reinvented in hues of tender reunion.
Westward, the horizon promises
all endings are merely origins.

Forsaken Hymn no. 91

In the silent stretch before dawn:
the world whispers its continuities,
roots wind deep in the dark loam,
grasping at the core of old stories,
   entwined: a mesh of life and decay.
What mysteries ferment beneath my sole,
each step a press on time's layered skin?

The air—sharp as flint—sparks
with the remnants of forgotten epochs,
and I, with my breath seen in puffs,
probe the chill that wraps its fingers tight.
   Branches crack like the bones of the earth,
breaking the silence with the sound of shifting;
each leaf a syllable in the ancient vocabulary

of growth, of death, of cycles spun anew.
   Here I stand, musing on the edge of the abyss,
ready to declare the resurrection of buried truths.
The soil whispers cold truths:
each grain, a story untold,
carved by the wind's tireless hands,
fixed in the cradle of roots.

Forsaken Hymn no. 92

The tulips widen: their petals sheer lengths,
stretching thin as if to breach their own confines:
   like ideas unfurling into the light, seeking
more than just the sun: a reason, perhaps,
for being so vivid against the spring's brush.
The clock ticks, each second a meticulous
sweep: the methodical pacing of time
that neither rushes nor waits for my consent.
Its gears, tight with precision, mimic

     the certainty I lack, the spirals of doubt
      that expand, contract, breathe.
     Outside, people pass: just silhouettes
against the flicker of life that continues
  despite my stasis. Their shadows dance
  on the walls of my confinement, lively
yet transient as a gust threading through
narrow leaves, whispering of places

both rooted and released.
    And as night descends, the stars—
those ancient lanterns of old navigators—
seem to whisper, in their distant flicker,
of travels beyond the tight, closed loop
of my own spiraling thoughts, urging
   a journey inward as deep and vast
     as any traversed space.

Forsaken Hymn no. 93

In the fading transitions of light:
this daily cycle of dawn to dusk,
atoms vibrate within the confines
of their molecular chambers:
our bodies, a universe echoing the vast,
swirling cosmos we strain to understand.

The entropy of age gathers,
unseen forces wearing down
the smooth stones of our vitality:
each wrinkle etched a line of wisdom,
each sigh a breeze over leaf-strewn paths,
    change: relentless, exhaled in silent beats.

What tales will I tell of gray twilights,
    the gentle decay of once vibrant blooms?
Life, a continuous thread woven through time,
stitching seconds into decades,
until all that remains are echoes of youth,
all cycles complete, quietly, wholly embraced.

Forsaken Hymn no. 94

Lines of life, drawn through the sterile air:
each breath a staccato of survival,
machines beep with a rhythm
that mimics the heart but not its essence.
In my veins, the slow drip of time
passes: chemical currents carving new paths.

   My eyes drift to the window, seeking
    the curve of the horizon: so distant,
     so closed off by walls that hold
the sterile whispers of this white sea.
Outside, trees must still heed the wind's call,
leaves fluttering in a dance of ongoingness.

Yet here, static clings to the corners,
where shadows speak more of dusk
than the light can reveal.
But in this suspension, I find a thought:
perhaps, in every ending, there is a start—
life, looping back, a continuous heart.

Forsaken Hymn no. 95

Each thought aligns, a delicate balance:
a leaf fluttering between wind gusts that
   whisper of chaos yet cradle precision—
the officer's gaze: sharp, dissecting,
   an entomologist pinning down the
flutter of my pulse beneath thin cloth.

   In this hard light, lines blur:
a uniform, stiff and starched,
  frames the man, his posture
both shield and condemnation,
   a boundary etched in woven fibers
that speak of order, a rigid lattice.

Yet within this grid, particles dance—
erratic as thoughts in feverish dreams,
where fear and respect mingle: drops
   of oil and water, refusing union
  but bound by the same vessel.
In the end, immutable laws govern us all.

Forsaken Hymn no. 96

Light filters through branches overhead:
   dawn splays its fingers wide,
    touching the cool, damp grass with a promise
of a sun-warmed day: such is the cycle,
perpetual yet each morning new,
   a paradox at the heart of the familiar.
The laughter of young scouts breaks

the heavy cloak of my solitude,
each footstep a beat in the earth's old heart,
   thumping a reminder of life's relentless parade.
  Their packs, not burdened with yesteryears,
swing with the easy rhythm of the unscarred.
  Yet, here I sit, a vessel of shadows and light,
pondering the depths of an ever-thirsty soul:

each drink a fleeting reprieve,
each dawn a reluctant salvation.
In this quiet, a dialogue with time,
I find peace a landscape, always rediscovered.
As the scouts disappear, their laughter still
echoes, a reminder of paths yet taken,
and paths too long avoided.

Forsaken Hymn no. 97

In the soft whisper of leaves: a chronicle,
etched in their veins, of seasonal shifts,
each leaf a page torn from time's own book,
and wind, the storyteller: an ancient voice
murmuring tales of growth, decay, renewal:
how energy flows, cycles: never lost, only transformed.

Beneath, the soil—rich with the compost
    of generations—holds tight the roots,
connections deep and dark as mystery,
feeding saplings with the wisdom
    of decayed forebears: life erected
on the remains: a fortress against entropy.

As dusk descends, shadows lengthen,
drawing thoughts to the close of day—
each sunset a soft closure, a gentle
shuttering of day's bright eye, giving way
to dark's embrace, where dreams ferment,
preparing us for the morrow's new breath.

Forsaken Hymn no. 98

In the hum of mingled voices, I watch:
   the arcs of his motion, once uncertain,
now deliberate, charged with the gravity
of realized dreams: how trajectory can shift,
    the span of one life reflecting the cosmos,
     a nebula bursting into being.

   His words weave through the clatter of cutlery,
an orbit of intent around old friends,
   reminding me: we are matter in motion,
subject to forces unseen, carving paths
through the dark matter of our doubts,
each step a declaration of change.

And as the night folds its tent,
   the gentle decay of light into memory,
I see in his ascent a parable of potential:
not bound by the hard molds of past judgments,
but free to explore, to expand, to exist,
redefining boundaries with every breath.

Forsaken Hymn no. 99

In the shadow of these temples, wind:
scarves of dust that swirl with myths,
  each grain a whisper of creation, disintegration:
  forces that carve canyons in the heart,
a geography of belief and doubt, alike:
  the landscape altering, never static.

Here, motion collides with stillness:
a priest, metallic roar cutting through prayer,
the abrupt engine stutters, then calms:
a juxtaposition—ancient stones and oil fumes,
leaking the sacred into air tainted by progress:
resistance, or embrace? The gods sigh.

Certainty dissolves like sugar in rain,
  questions fermenting like the sharp rhubarb,
its acid cleansing, biting back:
the sanctity of space, profaned yet held dear,
a temple, not merely stone but the span
between belief and the reverence of questions.

Forsaken Hymn no. 100

In the hush of predawn: quiet spectra rise,
   echoes of light on the horizon, blurring
notions of time: our shared, cyclic pulse.
The firmament whispers of origins,
ancient as her laughter in the sunlit
kitchen: each wrinkle, a story scribed.

   Cell by cell, the narrative weaves—a tapestry,
    wound from strands of resilience: endurance
crafted beneath her skin, tough as oak.
Photosynthesis: how she converts
pain to energy, sunlight to sustenance,
rooted deep in the loam of legacy.

   Our histories intersect like rivers at confluence,
each bend shaped by the relentless press
   of water over stone: the shaping of souls.
In her eyes, the reflection of starlight—
paths traced in the arch of skies,
   her strength completes its journey here.

Forsaken Hymn no. 101

The lake mirrors a fragmentary sky:
its surface, a canvas of fleeting reflections,
where egrets glide—pale strokes against the dusk,
each footfall stirring not just water, but thought.
I speak of dreams, fluid and unbound,
how they spill over the ridges of our minds.

Paths converge here, Mother: reality
and the imagined twist like vine and tree—
intertwined, inseparable in their dance,
  edges blurring where water meets the shore.
Your hand in mine, grip woven tight,
we navigate the sprawl of dream's terrain.

  A distant siren slices through the calm,
like sharpness of a last call at dusk.
  Egrets pause, their bodies tense as thoughts
of fleeted time: Tim, unarrived, bound
elsewhere, perhaps glimpsing shadowed lives,
our day closes—completes with whispered sighs.

Forsaken Hymn no. 102

Swans curve through liquid gold,
rippling the still pond: nature's craft
  at play amid decaying grandeur,
echoing ages slipped beneath silent waves.
The cycle turns: entropy meets renewal,
roots deep in the time-softened earth.

Our footfalls trace paths worn by whispers,
polyphonic rustling of leaves and timelines.
Each stone a chronicle, dense with the echo
of storied breaths: Delphi, Machu Picchu,
ghosts bound by the same perennial bind,
rising and falling like the chest of the day.

Here, amidst the philosophical quiet,
  our eyes harvest light, cobbling together
views from nature's yielding back.
We preserve: not just artifacts but pulses,
    her teeth, her truths, twisting through us,
  binding, letting go, ever toward dawn's renewal.

Forsaken Hymn no. 103

In the tremor of the hummingbird's flight,
its wings blur the line between science
and the magic of mere existence:
how does such weightless grace
  defy the heaviness of air,
    thread through the tight needle of survival?
Each hover: a soft pulse across
the spectrum of sunlight spooling

through chlorophyll veins: realities
  of green fused to gold in the fleeting
dance of daybreak and doppler shifts—
worlds within worlds, unseen, yet felt.
And so, muscles oscillate, unseen beneath
a shimmer that confounds the eye,
rapid as the heartbeat of atoms,
and I, rooted, unable to mirror

  such delicate velocity,
muse on the paradox of movement and stasis.
I think on these contrasts: the hummingbird
  and the sturdiness of my own bones,
anchored in the flux of time that flows
forward, ever forward, despite
the pull of past and potential—
    till silence sings, completing the year's circle.

Forsaken Hymn no. 104

The years peel back like birch bark:
   thin, revealing the tender under skin
of time—the striations in its build
   mark each season's shadow and glow,
each cyclical retreat into cold,
each blossom thrust into the spring air.

   Our faces bear the same pattern:
creases form where smiles broke,
the furrows from frowns, or squints
   at the sun—Archie's eyes carry a gleam,
a reflection of what was endured,
resilient against the scrape of years.

This path forward, woven between
   the known and unknown territories
of aged maps and fresh sketches,
might lead through wild, verdant growth:
each step a prayer, each breath a verse
written in the silence of hopeful continuance.

Forsaken Hymn no. 105

In the slow drift of continental plates,
the echoes of ancient discussions
   pulse through the root-web of oaks:
a democratic parliament of trees
      giving voice to myriad leaves
while monarchs, old as stone, hang heavy.

   Here, fluid as river currents, I find
my musings caught in the swirl:
democracy, like water, slips
through fingers clenched too tight,
and monarchy stands—stoic, crumbling—
in the relentless gale of change.

   In the classroom of life, we cast ballots
with the softest whispers of leaves,
deciding nothing, yet altering everything:
each choice a ripple in the pond,
      each belief a pebble in the stream,
until, at last, I rest in the flow, complete.

Forsaken Hymn no. 106

The breeze stirs: it whispers through cracked
paint: the porch sways: breath of the old house,
absorbing stories, like rings in a stump.
Each creak a footnote in nature's vast book,
  each nail rusted, each board warped, speaks of years,
    cycles of sun to frost to bloom again.

Leaves brush the ground: a soft, chaotic waltz,
    each twirl a measure of time, a fragment
  caught in the spin of earth's indifferent dance.
The pup, bandaged, sighs beneath my hand: pain
mingled with trust: the cycle of healing
slow but as sure as the sun's path across.

  As dusk deepens, the sharp contours of day
  blur into night's soft ambiguity.
Stars prick the sky, the eternal quiet,
  reminding me that all pain, all joy, is
mere dust in the universe's broad palm.
  Love whispers back from darkness: we endure.

Forsaken Hymn no. 107

In evening's quiet, creatures stir,
their masked faces probing, a dance
of nimble fingers through my world's
    detritus: a communion at dusk.
Each small hand, an exploration:
More than theft, a survival dance.

Their eyes, like small moons, catching fire
from my torchlight, a brief flaring
of kinship in the dimming glow.
Under the old crab tree, histories
merge: their wild roamings, my static watch,
two worlds spiraling towards a fold.

Yet, we dance this delicate waltz:
I, with my burdens, they, with their bold
curiosity, both caught in the relentless
pull of life's intricate weave.
From raccoon eyes to human heart,
we find our shared rhythm beneath the stars.

Forsaken Hymn no. 108

The hard ice cracks beneath my feet:
each step a sharp reminder: life is brittle,
yet each fracture sings of the strain and thaw,
the expansion and contraction of worlds
    within the water's frozen memory:
where winter's grasp tightens, resilience blooms.

Beneath the aged elm, icicles hold tight,
dangling like chandeliers, casting prisms:
light split into stories of spectral hues,
each droplet a universe, suspended,
    awaiting the melt to return it to the roots,
sustenance drawn deep from the chill.

This cycle, relentless as the seasons' shift,
echoes the warm breath of summer lost
    to the quiet white of winter's truth:
here, in this stillness, lies the pulse
of all that retracts to bloom again,
where cold's harsh lesson folds into spring's embrace.

Forsaken Hymn no. 109

Leaves crumble underfoot: a slow dance
of decay: brittle fragments whispering
their last, tethered to the cycle of return:
earth inhales them: rebirth pending.
Here, Archie watches: hopeful eyes
gleam against the somber hues of twilight:

a world receding yet pulsing anew
   in the tender belly of night: life
     stirring its faint, critical flame:
   next season's bloom silently shaped.
Seasons pivot on the axis of change:
   each leaf, each frozen petal, a testament

   to time's relentless swirl: we stand
   witness to the bloom and wilt:
our lives—fleeting shadows on the sunlit wall—
genres of endings we must embrace. In this,
the promise of spring whispers closure,
   soft as a sigh: renewal is the final grace.

Forsaken Hymn no. 110

In the dimming light of a fading day,
I stand where shadows stretch their long fingers
   over the crumpled truth, remembering
   how easily the blue and plain ones dissolve
into the fabric of my own darkening thoughts.
There is a disquiet in the air, a murmur

of deceit played out behind closed doors
where they feed on the vulnerable with lies
   spun as fine and treacherous as spider silk.
   The horizon blurs: a seamless blend
of earth and sky: nature's vague promise
   or threat, depending on the tilt of the mind.

The cycle spins, stars wheel their silent arcs,
roots delve deeper into the cold, unyielding earth,
grasping at the hidden waters: life's elixir.
Amidst this eternal rhythm, I find
a quiet assurance, a bound stability
that renders transient deceits into whispers.

Forsaken Hymn no. 111

This tundra breathes: each gust a verse,
    whispered from ice-lipped cracks and crags:
how slight the weight of human steps
in landscapes vast, indifferent.
    The cards scatter, black and red,
against the white: stark contrasts —
    like blood on snow: unforgotten,

yet absorbed by the hunger of cold.
    The stars overhead: indifferent judges,
aloof to the gambles beneath their gaze.
Each flicker, a heartbeat; each dimming,
a sigh from the cosmos's depths.

Memories tread softly here,
between the frozen layers of time:
    I sift them, like searching for
seeds in the sterile, endless white.
The sky does not care for our woes,
nor the snow for the warmth of truth.

Forsaken Hymn no. 112

The sky cracks open: a revelation
of light breaking through: that first shard
splicing the curtain of everyday grays,
highlighting the dust: particles, precise
as the atoms that dance in balletic discord:
   I think of her eyes then: how they hold stars.

In this moment, where breath syncs with wind,
each gust a page turned in the book of our days,
the leaves write in swirls—lost languages
   of green decay: her voice echoes back
across time's vast, impersonal plain—
her laughter: the mathematics of joy.

From within the interstice of her smile
to the steady press of her feet on earth,
paths unfold: ribbons of possibility.
   As she celebrates another circle of sun,
renewal: each year blooms from the last—
like seasons, she turns: complete, enduring.

Forsaken Hymn no. 113

In the cooling twilight, every leaf:
a whisper, the shadows casting tales
of spirits mingling:: their voices,
   soft and stark against the setting sun.
I tread lightly on the moss-carpeted ground,
each step sinking slightly, a quiet echo
of the divine's arbitrary touch on souls:

crushing, enlightening, yet perplexing.
Heartbound to earth, skybound in thought,
  the irony of divine mandates emerges:
corporeal bindings that release infinite flights,
where freedom and fate perform their tightrope dance.
Here amid ancient trunks, the air vibrates

with the subtle decay of fallen heroes:
My mother's grace, my father's stern eye,
symbols of a divine irony: harsh yet essential.
    A star pierces the evening's veil, reminding me
     of Archie's spirit, shackled yet soaring
beyond the grasp of celestial decrees,
  a testament to human endurance and folly.

Forsaken Hymn no. 114

Leaves rustle, a whisper at dawn's edge:
each quiver a signal, a collected history,
etched in veins that the wind reads:
nature's own script, inked onto the air.
Seasons shift, guided by unseen hands,
the world remakes itself in silent debates
on survival, on the growth that must follow

the shedding of the old: the inevitable cycle.
Here I stand, surrendering to this flux,
wondering at the simplicity of complexity,
how roots dig deep, draw sustenance
from layers unseen: the cold, dark earth.
Soil: a fabric woven with the bones
of the past, feeding the relentless future

with decay turned into life again:
this is the truth held in the dust.
    From beneath, the surge of renewal,
where every end folds into a beginning,
and I, a witness to the persistent pulse
of creation, find solace in the continuity.

Forsaken Hymn no. 115

In this bakery's dusky nook, shadows line the walls:
clouds of flour rise and settle
as she slides trays beneath the eager glass,
her movements smooth as a river's gesture,
   cupcakes and tarts, arrayed like fallen stars,
forgotten yet still aglow.

Her hands, seasoned in the art of letting go,
flit like moths against the dimming light:
   she does not flinch at the echo of doors,
or at dreams that pace, restless,
   in the cramped heart of paper stacks—
each page a quiet testament to persistence.

Outside, the sky prepares to weep its grace,
and inside, she measures out her smiles, sparingly,
like sugar rationed for a lean winter.
Here, in the weave of simple acts,
      the symphony of routine plays its notes—
her resilience, the melody that persists after the curtain drops.

Forsaken Hymn no. 116

Lichen clings to oak: slow union,
a melding quiet and sure, just as
   our words wander, catch on
the branches of argument,
then find clearer air for roots:
how the forest teaches—
   patience in layering moss,

the sudden fall of an aged limb,
   making space for light: how
   change grips, renews.
Understood in the silence,
  the fraternity of fungi and root:
whisper of water through rock,
   each droplet reshaping what it touches:

   all things in flux, but bound.
So, we speak, and speaking,
  weave the old and new,
   trust the ground to hold,
   the sky to listen: our breath
mingling with the pine, the earth.

Forsaken Hymn no. 117

In the sway of seasons, time bends:
stretched thin over the edges of maps,
    where hearts mark their uncertain territories,
each beat: a seismic whisper, a flutter,
a shared longitude of loss and discovery.
The wind, aloof archivist, records
each fracture in frostbitten leaves:

  it charts the chill retreat of warmth,
turning affection into artifact,
mirroring the fixed orbits of distant stars.
We, like continents drifting, inches apart,
  navigate the spaces that both divide and bind:
  following currents, stirred by unseen hands,
    pointing our compasses toward

the silent symphony of the heart:
here, where every ending begins anew.
In the frost of Archie's glance: lines –
crisp as the edges of winter leaves,
each contour marked by a starkness,
    where light fractures on icicle sheaths:

Forsaken Hymn no. 118

In the hush after cheers: quiet blossoms:
petals fold inward, hiding their boldest hues
from the glare of notice, from eyes that only
see what light reveals, not where shadows hold
true colors, mingling dust with dew,
   roots deep where no applause can reach.

Each breath : a leaf's tremble on the wind:
   each moment alone in the crush of adoration
feels like standing beneath a vast sky, touching
   the pulse of a star throbbed unseen:
these are the distances within,
spaces no cheer can cloud or close.

But solitude is a silent companion,
   walking through the clamor, unseen yet felt,
where each step leaves a print, soft and deep,
in the soil of the soul: these quiet refuges,
   where we meet ourselves, unadorned and clear,
and finally resonate with completeness.

Forsaken Hymn no. 119

the call to conform:
  how my reflection aligns or bends away
from the expectations cast in steel molds,
from the flux of faces, hours, moments lost
to the still sharpness of morning rituals:
shave, rinse, repeat: each stroke a clearing,

each clearing a story of years swept away
with the foam and the tiny, sacrilegious
    hairs that dare grow different each day:
is this not growth, too: the rebellion
of the body against the march of time,
      the silent assertion of change as inevitable,

as necessary as breath? In this mirror
I see not just a man, but the myriad paths
winding back to childhood, forward
into the unknown haze of years unrolled:
today, I choose which face to wear,
ready, at last, for the world outside.

Forsaken Hymn no. 120

In the penumbra of a setting sun,
    deciphering the sharp, bitter tang
of old leaves: nature's manuscript
is not written in plain, smooth lines
    but in the jagged break of branches,
in the silent labor of roots.

Under the microscope, life scurries:
    an ant carries the green shard twice its weight,
  finding its path through dirt, mapped
by the magnetic pulse of the unseeable—
    each step, a testament to quiet persistence,
a song sung beneath the threshold of hearing.

As twilight deepens, casting shadows
across the face of my quiet contemplation,
  I recognize this seamless passage:
from dusk to dark, an endless cycle,
each phase a brush stroke on the canvas
of being, finely drawn to a close.

Forsaken Hymn no. 121

Leaves murmur the twilight's cool,
their edges silvered in the failing light:
each leaf a small, whispering historian
documenting the soft, gradual encroachments
of night, as shadows lengthen and deepen,
   pulling at the frayed threads of day.

Yet, in this crepuscular hour, thoughts stray
to the permanence of rocky crags
and the transient caress of wind:
   how both shape the rugged landscape
    of the soul, carving deep canyons
with the relentless river of time.

So here I stand, a solitary figure
   enshrouded by the looming oaks
and the sprawling ferns, witnessing
the last vestiges of light flee westward.
In this quiet, I find a communion,
and with the final rays, closure.

Forsaken Hymn no. 122

Leaves rustle: whispers to the wind,
such are the tales of Archie, captured:
   in the grip of his own spiraling,
the soil: his thoughts, loosed upon
a fertile plain, yielding remains,
   not of harvest, but of wild, untended sprawls.

   The sun casts long shadows—
nature's sundial, marking time
on this quiet stage of afternoon introspection:
each tree, a testament to standing still
while life whirls in frenzied dance around it,
   Archie the leaf in that tempest.

  In the serene vs. the chaotic,
a discourse unfolds:
how much of this play is ours to script?
The garden knows the vine's embrace,
   its relentless quest to overrun,
yet, in surrender, finds a kind of order.

Forsaken Hymn no. 123

In the quiet morning, light slices:
    through the blinds, as if cutting
softly through the dense fabric
of today, or yesterday, or any
day laid bare on the hardwood
floor in shades of ephemeral warmth.

The sun moves, so does its shadow:
a slow dance across the surface,
reminding us of time's gentle decay.
    Each beam of light, a transient touch
that whispers of endings: life's brief
play of light and dark, etched deep.

And yet, there is a comfort here:
in knowing our place in the folds
    of an unending curtain, draped
across the stage of the universe.
    We are transient yet eternal in the
quiet glory of dawn's fleeting light.

Forsaken Hymn no. 124

Snow softens the jagged edge of the world:
its mute blanket, a cover for old sores,
  healing the loud scars of the earth,
where under, new life stirs, waiting
for the thaw, the return of buzzing life,
  of growth, of cycles known yet always fresh.

Archie's joy, a newborn cry in silence,
  spans the gap of raw human hopes;
each wail a proclamation:
freedom from the womb's embrace,
a breaking of bonds, as with a crowbar,
forcing open the future's gate.

The old rhythms persist, insistent,
within this fresh canvas stretch,
  lines drawn, then blurred by snow:
our tales, retold in these quiet moments,
    where each ending folds back to its beginning,
and new life whispers of ageless continuities.

Forsaken Hymn no. 125

The clickety-clack of my iMac keyboard, quiet:
nature outside spins the louder wheel,
  its cycle unbroken by our digital intrusions.
For us, the screen light—our pale sun;
trees whisper through data streams,
    connecting root to pixel in a virtual mesh.

Ancient bards knew the cold bite of wind,
their chants woven with the harsh warp of storm:
  contrast this—our climate-controlled verses—
warm rooms tempering the edge of thought.
Is the spirit of verse diluted in comfort,
    or does it merely sleep, awaiting our awakening?

We trade immersion for interpretation,
seeking depths in the shallows of pages and posts:
    yet, beneath these calm surfaces,
the old currents run dark and deep.
In quiet moments, the soul stirs,
    reflecting, always, the pull of relentless tides.

Forsaken Hymn no. 126

In the pause of twilight, each breath:
a blend of shadow and sigh,
  the sky looped in the hues of cessation,
our lives: brief spirals in the vast dusk,
echoes trapped in marble and lore,
history's weight sealing the lips of the past.

  What finds its shape in this twilight exile?
Lines etched deep as if by time's own hand,
the cold touch of stone that remembers more
than we can tell: stories lodged in the fractures,
each name a held note in the silent hymn,
our days counted like stars fading at dawn.

  Yet, beneath these engravings, the earth shifts,
imperceptible, patient, crafting new legends,
as roots thread silently through ancient dust,
  the ceaseless whisper: everything changes,
  and we, standing on the precipice of memory,
    glean from the stones a firmer place to stand.

Forsaken Hymn no. 127

Leaves rustle: whispers at dusk,
their crisp voices chattering tales
of endings: how the world cycles
around the sun: seasons shift:
predictable yet ever new.
    Each leaf: a small spectral spirit
adrift amid the cool breath of fall,

hovering between life: its vivid flush,
and the quiet of decay: subtle, slow,
a vanishing into the soil's dark hold.
In this room, the air thickens
with shadows: long fingers stretching,
    reaching out from corners, whispering
of thresholds crossed, of the fine line

    between holding fast: and letting go.
    Outside, the moon, a pale witness,
charts the passage of another soul,
while inside, we navigate grief's quiet maze,
searching for signs, for words,
that might anchor us a moment longer.

Forsaken Hymn no. 128

In the fold of dusk: earth cools, exhales,
dew forms: the night's silver lining,
  each leaf a tiny mirror reflecting
    the imminent star-pricked darkness;
yet in this nightly passage, life persists:
tiny breaths, whispers of existence.

Processes hidden as roots delve deep,
  molecules dance with the fervor of ions,
    breaking, making bonds: the silent alchemy
that fuels the pulsing heart of a seed,
destined to break through, stretch toward
dim light, growing in the shadow of giants.

This cycle, eternal, etched in the spiral
of a snail shell: logarithmic precision,
a Fibonacci sequence in pine cone scales:
all nature's subtle, persistent calculation,
  guiding the chaos of creation toward
a simple, profound coherence: we endure.

Forsaken Hymn no. 129

The threads of the past intertwine
softly: the raw fibers of an untold
   story, pulling, loosening, falling
  into the patterns of nature's embrace,
    where each particle, vibrating,
holds a universe within.

   Echoes of Archie's laughter ripple
  through the still air: a reminder
   that matter neither vanishes nor
yields easily to the quiet, but shapes
the spaces left behind:
life's indelible impression.

In this twilight, our hands—once
clammy with youthful play—now
grasp only memories woven
in the loom of relentless time.
I reach for solace in the thought
of transformation: an unending cycle.

Forsaken Hymn no. 130

in the chill of the moment: electrons spin,
propelled by forces unseen yet deeply
  felt: much like sorrow, a natural fact,
a pull as real as gravity: binding us,
    together, or tearing apart:
    the roots of a tree exposed by wind.

    And there, in the midst of decay, life
insists, resilient: spores to fungi,
buds to blooms: transformations
    mirrored in the wounds that mark
  us, seasons shifting:
flora in relentless pursuit of light.

From this, perhaps, a broader spectrum:
    everything connected: the flow of blood,
  the cycle of cells, death giving way
to new growth: no final stroke,
just endless conversation:
    we are, after all, a part of that whole.

Forsaken Hymn no. 131

In the early haze of dawn, I spy:
    microscopic dew, the world encapsulated
in each droplet, life force magnified:
a universe held within a fragile sphere.
My thoughts scatter like spores,
released to the wind, each bearing a sliver
of my fractured peace, searching

    for fertile soil, a place to root:
and grow beyond the confines of chaos.
In the untamed garden of my mind,
    ideas sprout wild, invasive,
climbing the trellis of my sanity
with thorny questions: how does one cultivate

balance: when the seeds of doubt flourish?
I prune my fears, trim back the overgrowth
of tomorrow's anxieties, find solace
in the simple act of breathing, of being
    here, in this moment, where certainty
    is as transient as the morning fog.

Forsaken Hymn no. 132

In the twilight's murmur, night's weave:
a quiet between starlight and leaf rustle,
where debates of light and shadow
   cast stories on the old oak's skin:
each line a narrative, deep-grained,
history whispered through the corridors of sap.

How the cosmos spins, a silver dance
across the fabric of a sky so vast,
and we, mere echoes of a heartbeat's pulsar,
feel the push of wind, the pull of tides,
   gravities that hold yet free us,
   linking atom to the orb in celestial ballet.

Thus, in the simple silence after rain,
      the soil sends scents, rich and pungent,
breathing out the day's heavy heat
      in whispers: here we are, always becoming,
         never gone: our stories, like water, cycle—
from cloud to drop to stream to ocean.

Forsaken Hymn no. 133

Through the lens, a blurred grace:
    molecules dancing in the dim glow,
a flash captures the unsteady whisper
of my voice: a leaf in the torrent
    of ever-unfolding fame.
In this choreography of shadows and lights,
the constant hum of narrative weaves

    through my thoughts like ivy: invasive,
yet strangely anchoring this structure
of self, constructed from echoes
of someone I was told to be.
Yet, there is calm in the cyclical pulse,
the repeated arcs of lights dimming,
    the quiet that comes after the applause

drifts away into the cool evening air.
In that silence, I find a forgotten freedom,
my own voice amidst the fading echoes.
    In the small breaths between the clicks of a camera,
life persists: molecules bind and break,
the unseen mechanics of the world unfold:

Forsaken Hymn no. 134

In this slow dawning: how cells divide,
awaken under pressure, the relentless
push-pull of the waking world: my muscles
groan, fibers complain loud in the silence
before the chalk talks, the schoolyard calls.
Atoms, too, must feel this stretch, the bond strain
within the molecule's heart: where forces

meet and part: nature's soft lecture on
endurance, on the persistence found
in the throes of daily transformation.
Today, like Morse code: a signal pulsing
from the heart's tired chambers, tapping out
a rhythm: keep going, the whisper winds
through the corridors of thought: a quiet

hurricane, reshaping what will remain.
Waves break, reforms: and in the classroom, eyes
glisten like fresh dew on the verge of
evaporation: I stand, not just a teacher,
but a bridge, a moment's peace, connecting
curiosity with the known universe.

Forsaken Hymn no. 135

In the quiet, thoughts tread softly:
    like a cat's careful step around the periphery,
each whisker-twitch informed by starlight and shadow:
    how light splits the darkness, yet never displaces it,
an illustration of the balance between presence
and absence: a dance, a drift, a shift of cosmos.

Atoms whirl in their orbits, silent in their frenzy,
each collision an act that predicates a story,
    like the gentle, inevitable erosion of rock
    by a stream's persuasive whisper:
how the water shapes the stone,
    and the stone guides the stream.

In this room, where tales of fracture echo,
I am reminded that each breaking is also a making:
from the shards, new configurations,
    a mosaic crafted from splinters of old selves.
And in this light, where dust motes dance,
    understanding settles softly, complete and still.

Forsaken Hymn no. 136

In quiet turns: the world outside, a raging,
unaware of hushed interiors, where thoughts
spin: a rabbi's life quivers like a leaf
touching both fire and forebear echoes: old texts
   hold more than words: they cradle raw striving,
and the shadows that dance deep in flame.

His ink, a slow distillation: it drops
   heavy—each word a world, each pause a cosmos—
while outside, life demands, ever hungry,
   ever loud: her steps sync to survival's pulse,
each motion a script in the daily sacred,
   each breath a chapter in their joint tome.

Here, the wrestle with silence and clamor
binds softly: devotion's intricate lace,
overlaying duty's steadfast canvas:
   in this study, a universe whispers,
composing the unseen, essential hymns—
a closure woven through infinite loops.

Forsaken Hymn no. 137

Mornings unfurl: subtle light traces
the contours of what we think enduring,
an archway's shadow over the dew-soaked soil,
morning glories twine around the crumbling
relics of yesterday's grandeur: temples
that now breathe silence rather than chants.

This decay whispers of permanence
as a misnomer, nature reclaiming
its plotted land: vines creeping, wrapping
steel and stone alike, pulling them
gently, inevitably, back into the fold
of earth's indifferent embrace.

And in this soft surrender, a truth:
we are but visitors here, crafting
temporal homes in the sands of time,
each grain a testament to the transient,
our lives a brief reflection in the endless
cycle of bloom and wither, gain and loss.

Forsaken Hymn no. 138

I walk through a shadowed forest of neurons,
pondering: each leaf a thought, each branch
   a decision, sprouting: divergent pathways
where the roots grapple with soil:
rich in mineral-dark dilemmas,
holding water, holding secrets.

Sunlight filters through the canopy:
a flicker, a fleeting clarity
on the oscillating edge of uncertainty:
where photons collide and scatter,
like doubts in the gust of reason,
each one a small epiphany.

In this tangled undergrowth,
each step is a new hypothesis,
testing the firmness of the earth:
how delicate the balance,
   how meticulous the chaos,
how profound the quiet closing.

Forsaken Hymn no. 139

Mist wraps the hills: early light diffused
by the burden of history's weep.
    Silver threads drift from the ancient tower,
    calling out to a prince long lost
in the echoes of a question: why did he leave?
    Heartlines traced through the damp earth's scent.

Every leaf, a silent witness to cycles
of growth and decay: microcosms
reflecting the Escherian stairs of human folly.
Where love spirals, inevitability looms:
a lore of roots entwined yet asunder,
    the cold embrace of dew on a spider's web.

In the threshold's shadow, I pause:
    holding the weight of door neither closed nor open.
    The veils of time shift, revealing
glimpses of past passions, tangled and torn.
And in the quiet dissolve of dusk,
I find my answer, whispered by the wind: he never truly left.

Forsaken Hymn no. 140

The light breaks early, clear and cold:
it pierces through the frailty of aged oaks,
splintering bark, life held tight in the gnarled
grip of years: how deeply run the roots
in dark, unseen spaces where whispers
of decay are only that: whispers.

The creek, too, knows this silent fray
between the pressing ice and stubborn stone,
   its waters a testament to the persistence
of movement: erosion, an eternal artist,
sculpting cold pathways through unyielding
matter, mimicking the flow of time itself.

We talk of permanence as if we own it,
    as if our breaths aren't borrowed from the wind,
   our bodies not merely vessels for the briefest
    sparks against the vast, indifferent night.
In this, the quiet unraveling, I find solace:
    Archie knows, and so must I, all things conclude.

Forsaken Hymn no. 141

Snow packs down, firm beneath my boots:
hollow crunch, keen air slices—
such purity in the squeeze of cold,
compression: life distilled to crystal:
   the breadth of space shrinks, contracts,
Archie's breath, a fog before him.

Each step stirs the silent field—
thoughts alight like birds scattered
by winter: restless, seeking shelter.
This landscape: a canvas,
white stretches, untarnished yet
heavy, with the weight of waiting.

Survival: not just endurance but essence:
   Archie, whose days become effort,
who knows the keen edge of solitude,
finding in each icicle a sharp reminder
of the need to persist, to provide:
here, in the cold, the heart finds its warmth.

Forsaken Hymn no. 142

In the soft blush of twilight hours,
where silence blooms like night flowers,
echoes ripple: laughter gone,
yet their faint whispers linger on:
a tapestry woven with threads of jest,
now a silent hall, the mind's contest.

   Across the vast, dim-lit expanse,
     shadows dance—their dark romance
a play of light, a flicker, a pause:
the heart flutters, caught in the claws
of desires, the beast roams freely within,
tethered by vows, a thin, fragile skin.

And here, in the quiet echo of choice,
a muted voice finds its rejoice:
resisting, persisting against the sweet tempt,
where weakness and fortress are equally dreamt.
   I stand, the river of conscience wide,
flowing to truths, where peace resides.

Forsaken Hymn no. 143

In the hush of dusk, oak leaves whisper
secrets of the soil: each grain, its saga;
life cycles spiraling from the deep
earth, stirring roots to outstretch,
yearn towards the receding sun,
the calm tragedy of light fading
yet promising return: how similar

to the love harbored across time,
unseen but felt, like groundwater
nourishing the hidden seed,
beneath these boughs, my mind wanders,
through memories, stark and soft,
grasping at the echoes of laughter
and tears, that which sustains

and that which devastates; here,
I find a silent solace, embraced by nature's arm.
Beneath this old, gnarled oak: my refuge,
where leaves whisper histories,
the sun dips, a ball of fire into the sea—
nature's own performance in brilliant decay.

Forsaken Hymn no. 144

In the garden, under the cold gaze of the moon,
    leaves rustle: a quiet summons to witness
    their dance with the inevitable frost.
The boughs sag, heavy with ripened pears:
    each drop a punctuation in the narrative
of renewal, decay, and the relentless cycle.

Layered beneath, the soil harbors seeds,
waiting: their stillness not absence but
a form of patience, attuned to the whispers
of time. Roots delve in darkness, reaching,
    finding nourishment in memory and matter,
connecting the seen to the unseen.

    Through this simple scenery, I discern
    the vast weave of continuance: how even
the dying leaf fuels the living earth,
how each ending crafts a beginning, adherent
    to the promise of a cycle: seamless,
        where even in departure, we find return.

Forsaken Hymn no. 145

Light breaks: the dawn shifts its weight,
  shifting hues on the horizon's pale face:
the day begins with the minutiae of warmth,
spreading over the edges of the world,
a slow rendering of the night's cold grip:
nature's inexorable pulse, a canvas laid bare.

Spheres spin: an echo in the void,
the quantum dance of particles unseen,
binding the fabric of a universe stretched wide,
   over distances immeasurable by the simple compass
of human understanding or a father's silent choice:
each atom aligned in the grave geometry of loss.

And so, we are left: stitching hope into voids,
   tracing constellations in our fractured reflections,
  each star a story of fire and fading glory
  as we navigate by their given light, dim but steady,
the paths not taken, the roads forged by solitude:
in the starlit silence, an understanding, whole at last.

Forsaken Hymn no. 146

Leaf-shadows play: the sun, a filtered guest,
weaves through the branches, a tapestry
of light and dark: how intricate the dance
between what thrives and what merely survives:
yet, all is transient, flowing like water,
or thoughts through the unquiet mind.

Granite underfoot, cold, unyielding:
it records nothing of our passage,
unlike the forgiving soil: time's witness,
silent yet speaking in sediments and roots:
each layer a chapter, heavy with stories,
every grain an echo of old truths:

So we ponder, feet planted, heads in clouds,
our breaths a mist mingling with the winds:
do we not also dissolve, our features
etched away by the elements of days?
Yet in this moment, here is eternity—
the final note that lingers, resonates.

Forsaken Hymn no. 147

ephemeral, fleeting:
  yet in this momentary dance of shadows,
the leaf, once tethered, spirals free—
its descent caught in the quiet breath
    between hypothesis and law:
  a testimony to the pull of earth, the grip
of unseen forces shaping our very bones,

sculpting sinews like riverbeds eroded
by persistent waters from timeless rains:
here, where science meets the spirit,
    the dance commingles: elements and essence,
spinning a web from which none may detach,
  yet within which all remains singular,
untouched yet wholly integrated:

in the drift of particles, a universe hums,
  echoing the vast, immutable cycles
that bind decay to rebirth,
dark to light, finite to infinite:
in every ending, a genesis whispers,
breathing life back into the void,
restoring music to silent chambers:

Forsaken Hymn no. 148

Each moment unfolds: a leaf in descent,
whispering through the still autumn air
and landing, a soft fact, upon the earth,
  its details rich in the decay.
Lives, too, are sedimentary: layering,
the past pressed deep by the weight of the new,
    each layer: a story's subtle sieve

filtering sunlight and shadow alike.
Here, in this room: the quiet accumulates,
dust motes dancing in the shaft of light—
ancient sunlight captured then let go,
a spectral analysis of time.
Atoms, like words, bond and break:
ephemeral architectures,

each bridge burned illuminating
another way across the river.
The room pivots on the axis of light,
revealing the geometry of lost afternoons.
Outside, the world proceeds: cycles of growth
    and decay mirroring these internal tides.

Forsaken Hymn no. 149

Each memory spins: a leaf in the wind:
away from the stem, into the vast, blue above.
How the sunlight used to break on his laughter,
fragmented, yet whole in its brief echo.
Now shadows fold between books and walls,
the silence thick as molasses.
   We talked, words rich as soil,

till dusk sifted through the open window.
   We shaped our dreams with the hands of clock,
each tick: a stitch in time: someday to be undone.
Atoms, they bind and break, so did our paths,
   his voice now a hum in the heart's recess.
I trace the contour of our past,
   fluid as river meandering to sea.

Every remembrance a sediment laid down:
   the years erode, but leave outlines distinct.
   His absence—a cavity in the earth,
resonant with what fills the void:
   silence, then, is not empty, but thick
with echoes: every end cradles beginnings.

Forsaken Hymn no. 150

The city breathes: exhales of steam
and whispers, a surge of atoms
colliding in vast emptiness:
how spaces fill with the unseen,
    the unnoticed, the once-heralded man
now shadows his past in quiet retreat.

This puzzle of light and withdrawal—
the bright flare of youth dims
to the murmur of aged isolation,
    echoes in the canyons of stone and loss:
where does brilliance reside
when the street's applause ends?

Each corner, a story untold,
each face, a chapter closed in the dim light,
and here, amid ceaseless tides of movement,
he finds no comfort, no firm ground,
    only the soft whisper of the city night:
all things must merge into the one from whence they sprang.

Forsaken Hymn no. 151

In the silence where we stand: the air still,
heavy as if bearing the weight of unseen atoms,
   history's invisible hand guides our mourning—
each of us entangled in a network of loss,
the fine threads of connection glistening
like dew on a spider's spun web at dawn.

   Through this quiet grove, echoes speak:
the rustle of leaves, a soft lamentation,
    whispered secrets of decay and renewal,
the cycle that spins relentlessly onward,
atoms to dust, grief to understanding,
a cosmos indifferently nurturing its own.

In the spiraling galaxy of our shared sorrow,
each star a story, extinguished yet radiant,
we find in this communion a gentle closure,
the peace of knowing he rests within the vast,
   forever a part of the all-encompassing dark,
    and we, under the same stars, carry onward.

Forsaken Hymn no. 152

In the rustle of old leaves underfoot:
I hear the whispers of our past discourse,
   thoughts once vibrant, fading into the hush
of autumn's crisp inevitability.
   Life cycles: photosynthesis to decay,
atoms in endless rearrangement:
such is the nature of our fleeting days,

patterns persisting in perpetual flux.
   Each stride a brushstroke on nature's canvas,
   painting memories on the path to where
shadows lengthen and the soft light lingers:
The Latin prof's house stands silent, bearing witness.
   Here, where inspiration's wild flames leapt,

caught off-guard by the ferocity
   of sudden insight, or slow-dawning truths,
the future seemed not ours to question, but
   to shape with bold strokes and bright colors,
      untamed by the somber grasp of twilight.

Forsaken Hymn no. 153

Beneath the indifferent span of sky,
the sun, a fading sovereign, draws veils
of weary gold across the dying day:
    so ends another scene in nature's play,
  where randomness holds sway in divine jest,
    and entropy kisses each crest and trough.

Each tree, a whisper in the cosmic gust,
speaks of cycles, unasked and unfulfilled,
and leaves flutter down, knowing not the why,
only that the time comes for them to fly:
    sand through the glass, so time slips, grain by grain,
a melody wrought in the key of change.

Yet, here I stand, rebel to fate's harsh song,
  defying the silence left in stars' wake.
  The universe expands, indifferent,
    but in its vastness, a spark: we persist,
  defiant, casting shadows against the void,
knowing even stars are destined to fade.

Forsaken Hymn no. 154

Morning shadows stretch, thin and reaching,
over bare floors where dust speckles light:
   each grain, a tiny cosmos spinning in silent arcs,
      mirroring the vast orbits of our tangled lives.
Connections thread through the maze of existence,
binding us, breaking us: human conditions
that map our spirits, linking us to each other,

yet pushing us, too, toward our lonely precipices.
In the raveled edges of trust, how we fray,
the weft of our relationships undone
by threads pulled by wary hands,
   suspicion: a subtle, steady pull unraveling fabric.
Darkness at the edges of friendship cries out,
   the midnight call, a voice crackling through ether,

not just a bridge but a plea,
stirring the quiet room with echoes of despair.
A man, once a beacon, now shadowed by doubt,
   his name a whispered curse in corridors
once filled with laughter and shared secrets,
     how quickly the bright tapestry fades.

Forsaken Hymn no. 155

Amid his tumult: veins that mapped skies
clouded over; his gait, a quaking earth,
with each step, a genesis: stirring depths
where the dark sediment of his soul
floats dislodged, suspended and unseen:
a cosmos yielding to entropy.

His eyes – mirrors of a storm's heart
caught in the loop of lightning, flickering;
his voice – a bough snapping in the wind:
his words fractured, dispersing like light
in water: each moment glistening, fleeting:
   a delicate scattering of truths.

   I watch, breathless, as the morning
unfurls: the sun drags shadows
from beneath his tired eyes, outlining
   what's left: the stark silhouette of peace:
a quiet house, the cease of winds—
an echo fades, grounding us both.

Forsaken Hymn no. 156

In the chill morning, dew beads on grass:
   a universe in each droplet,
reflecting the vast webs, connections:
the spaces between not empty but
   pulsing with the unseen, life's quiet force:
      paths atoms wander, drawing near, apart.

This, the science of loss, the physics of sorrow:
every ending a transformation,
matter shifting states, spirits slipping free:
how could he be gone when energy
does not vanish—merely changes shape,
a continuity that physics promises.

Yet emotions tally no equations,
the heart knows no conservation laws:
each memory a star fading from night's tapestry,
yet, in these pages, his words persist—
   lines that bind us beyond the pulse of days:
      and in them, he finds a way to stay.

Forsaken Hymn no. 157

Through dashes of sun, light leaks in:
rippling across the creek's gentle swell
where waters murmur the old truths,
  how all is fleeting, even brilliant stars
burn out, their light echoing in voids,
distances vast, yet reachable, like thoughts.

Each song I wrote, a universe expanding:
  pressure of creation, heavy as gravity,
pull of orbit around the memory –
a life traced in the lines of melody,
binding spirit and matter,
where music meets quantum threads.

Now, in these quiet woodland breathes,
  I sense his presence in the chorus
  of leaves: whispers of spectral melodies,
notes flutter on breezes, timeless,
connecting us in a symphony
just as real as any touch could be.

Forsaken Hymn no. 158

The horizon stretches, vast and empty:
    between us, distances grow, not just in miles,
    but in the quiet moments we once shared,
now echoing back in the pulse of absence.
Each goodbye: a leaf fallen, the tree still stands;
its roots, though unseen, clutch tightly to earth,
    embracing change that comes with each new sun,

a cycle of growth, decay, and rebirth.
    And yet, as the dawn awakens afresh,
so does the memory of forest walks,
your laughter filtering through the canopy,
light fracturing on the moss below.
Time continues its relentless march, footfalls
soft on the path that leads you to new starts,

leaving behind the comfort of known trails:
each step a bridge to futures yet uncharted.
As the winds shift, carrying you beyond,
know this: the seed of your past is sown deep
    in the fertile soil of our collective being,
nurtured by the waters of shared dreams.

Forsaken Hymn no. 159

In the shadow of the slanting sun,
where the edges of day blur:
Archie's hands, untying, confess
to the loosened silk, slipping free,
the last light catching the unraveled threads,
each a pathway leading away.

The fabric of time folds upon itself,
    each crease a story half-told:
my heart beats—irregular, untamed—
    a syncopated rhythm mirroring
the pulsing quietude of a sunset
dyed in the hues of half-remembered dreams.

As the horizon swallows the sun,
and shadows blend into emerging stars,
I find the courage in the dimming glow
to let go of what I cannot hold:
the truth lies in the unraveled tie,
the story complete in its final fold.

Forsaken Hymn no. 160

In this crepuscular age, I note:
   the nature: how it bends and shapes,
each leaf a testament to the resilience
required for survival: fractals
   in the veins, like rivers seen from space,
   destined paths laid by untouchable hands.

Through my window: a scene
   of deliberate slow-motion: trees
swaying, philosophical in their stoic dance,
   roots deep in thought, anchored
in dark earth's nurturing bosom:
   their quiet wisdom seeping into my study.

Here, amid papers littered like fallen leaves,
the fire's warm flicker contends
with encroaching shadows: outside, twilight deepens,
inside: the quiet stir of memory,
   affections, smoldering, not yet ash,
calm in their glowing, enduring embrace.

Forsaken Hymn no. 161

within this town: its history measures
more than simple years: it breathes
in limestone seams and carven in echoes,
shadows cast by sunlight at three—
intersecting: the lives of saints
with the daily bread of bakers,
here, where leaf veins trace

pathways, reminiscent of stained glass—
innovations borne on winds and whims:
each cobblestone: a footprint
  overlapped; centuries whisper:
  turn not away from the minor
details: for therein lies the truth
of existence: molecules and mantras

intertwined, like roots clenching soil—
and how does the ground speak?
  Through each emerging sprout, biology—
a testament to time's unfailing urge
to press forward, generate: life cycles
closing, at seasons' sublime decree.

Forsaken Hymn no. 162

The pond reflects a somber sky:
mirrored gray that whispers of
   distant tumults, the churn of
far-off lands, fingers dipped
in murky waters, stirring the
   silt of agendas and strife.

Morning brings the paper, heavy
with the dead: numbers
etched in columns, lives
compressed to data, cold as
the monks' fire is hot: a stark,
burning protest, a beacon.

  What dragon lies not in myth
but in the veiled thrusts of power,
   his breath corrupting truth with
  smoke, teaching hate through
obscured glass? Under the open sky,
peace remains a shadow, fleeing.

Forsaken Hymn no. 163

In this dimming light, shadows deepen:
what does it mean, to be full, or merely fed?
The oak leaves tremble, a cool whisper,
as if to say that survival is not the same
as thriving: essence tucked beneath bare effort.
The creek babbles, a constant undercurrent,
its flow charting a path set by smoother stones,

unseen, yet felt—a course shaped
    by the pressures of soft soil, hard rain,
and the resistance of its own banks:
continuance despite the easy give of earth.
So, too, do I trace my own patterns—
how many times have I rounded this bend?
  The evening chills, a crispness steals in,

reminding me of the cycle: seed, sprout,
    reap, rest—each season, a fresh ledger.
As the last light lingers on the horizon,
    I think of Archie: steadfast as the oak,
    his roots tangled in the richness
    of a soil too tough to simply nurture.

Forsaken Hymn no. 164

Amid winter's grasp, life pauses: seeds
beneath the freeze ponder the cold's necessity,
    roots tangled in a frost-locked dance:
  they wait for the thaw, for the signal
that spirals from the sun's distant furnace,
waking the sleeping geraniums, the dormant buds.

The path of sap, unseen yet vital, mirrors
    our own hidden streams of thought:
flowing deep where eyes can't follow,
nourishing faint stirrings beneath
    the bark, the skin, a quiet pulse
in the dark earth, in the veined wrist.

Each season, a script: written, erased:
the sky reconfigures its clouds, memories
altered with each shift of wind; and I,
  reflecting the transient sky, find solace
    in the cyclical chant of creation—
where all endings are, indeed, beginnings.

Forsaken Hymn no. 165

The night, vast as the cosmos, envelops me:
  orange moon—silent witness to my fragment,
echoing Archie's fractured humerus,
his arm a metaphor for deeper breaks.
    Each wave whispers of unity and loss,
the sea's calm surface, a deceitful mirror.

Reflections ripple, distort under moonlight,
each pulse a story of what was, what's changed.
My body, a traitor, now seeks to mend
broken bones, sinew, while the soul yearns
for wholeness in the fracture,
  a peace amidst the storm of quiet despair.

In this solitude, the moon's cold flame guides,
burning with secrets of rejuvenation.
Like Archie, I contemplate a journey,
not across seas but through self,
accepting the incompleteness as whole—
finding in broken places, a new kind of perfect.

Forsaken Hymn no. 166

As I tread lightly: the fallen leaves whisper:
each step is a dialogue with earth's memory:
held in the damp soil, the roots transmit
signals: deep, where taproots embrace rock,
and fine hairs sip the dusk's dew delicately:
    above, the canopy strains in a wind not felt below.

The pursuit of genesis, a spark in twilight,
leads me along whispered paths: molecules,
    energy, diffusing through sinew and leaf:
    my eyes, clouded as a misted dawn, still see
how light wends through minute gaps:
particles colliding, reflecting, existing briefly.

What home, this? Fabricated not of stone,
but of echo and response: I find my footing
in the hum of the understory, thick with life,
each breath a stitch in time's vast quilt:
here, ears attuned to the quietest shifts,
resting at last, knowing the voyage circles here.

Forsaken Hymn no. 167

Amid the quiet chaos of connection,
papers scatter, autumn's own disciples:
each a testament written in the veins
   of organizational life, the pulse and pause
of systems: legal, financial, intertwined.
  The rustling secrets, they whisper:
fragments of the vast, the innumerable,

    held by mere fiber, seen through the haze
   of morning's reluctant illumination,
pondering simplicity lost, evolution gained.
From youthful rhythms to adult's echo,
   the once and thrice of mails, now replaced
by digital bursts, instant yet hollow,
  our exchanges fast yet distant, a paradox

    in the palm—connectivity's double edge.
The solidity of paper anchors longing,
each envelope a potential revelation,
   a tactile bridge over isolating expanse,
  craving past's immediate touch,
how we yearn, yet adapt, to shifting sands.

Forsaken Hymn no. 168

In this dim room: shadows stretch—
taut lines across old wooden floors,
whispers pool beneath the door
echoing betrayal's sharp clang.
The new figure, dark, large, unknown
fills spaces with unfamiliar presence,
  fear and love, strangely entwined,

  mingling like oil and water, unresolved,
  never mixing, but ever there:
the complex dance of new kinship.
  The echoes of a friend's betrayal linger,
a knife's memory fresh, cold,
sour milk, honey lost to harsher times.
Touches that once seemed tender

  now brand with unseen marks,
the sting of invisible slaps etched within.
  Lost promises play out in absurd cacophony,
every turn mocking the sacred once held.
  Amid it all, the Cross stands, stark,
a stark reminder of sacrifices, forsaken hopes.

Forsaken Hymn no. 169

In the dim light, books pile high:
histories of vanished empires,
novels filled with whispered love,
science texts, cracked and dry:
each page a testament to the thirst
  for knowing, arching beyond the dust.

Surrounded by these tomes and thoughts,
    my mind darts from the swollen ankles
to the broad sweep of wars outside,
where words wrestle with the rifles:
can a poem shield a heart, or a story
    turn the tide of human ache?

Here, within these cluttered walls,
each object poised for a journey—
a razor, silent and sharp like fate,
shirts folded, ready to face the front,
books that bridge the intimate and infinite—
all weaving a tapestry of tentative peace.

Forsaken Hymn no. 170

Weight of words, like stones in pockets:
why cling to this sinking? Pressed
into the depths, where critique's cold current
sweeps away the warmth of candid breath,
here: to withdraw, boarding my solitary craft
on the expanse of a less charted stream.

Sail set to catch the wind unburdened by
the heavy lexicon of old arguments, twirled
by simpler narratives that web across the vast,
unknowing sky: such liberty in the displacement
of dense air by my own unscripted sighs,
quietly defying gravity's pull.

Amid this freeing breadth, my vessel glides—
    forward, under the arch of endless horizons,
each wave a new thought, unweighted,
unwound from the tight coils of norm.
Here, my words drop into the ocean,
    simple, pure, completing my unbound script.

Forsaken Hymn no. 171

In this quiet room: her essence spills
over the bounds of the ordinary,
like light sifting through cracked amber:
her laughter resonates, a soft melody
carried on the breeze: it whispers
of secrets, shared beneath vast, starry canvases.

Her steps, small cascades of rhythm,
echo in my thoughts, wavelets lapping
at the shores of my consciousness:
    she is the pull of moon on tide,
the subtle force that guides
the sea's relentless return to land.

    In each contour of her form, I trace
the arc of planets: her gestures,
a gravity that binds like atoms entwined:
and in this cosmic dance—her smile
    haloes her face: I, suspended in awe,
find the universe, at last, perfectly aligned.

Forsaken Hymn no. 172

In the leaf's vein, the science of living:
each pattern a narrative, writ in green ink,
　　mapped out: the structure of breath, photosynthesis,
sunlight transformed into a pulse beneath bark.
Roots, like thoughts, stretch out, searching,
holding earth's mysteries deep in their clasp;
the soil that feeds also anchors,

a paradox: the freedom found in being bound.
　　Leaves whisper of growth and decay,
cycles that spin, relentless yet graceful:
each fall a farewell, each budding a hello,
constant in change, like waves in their ebb.
　　The wind speaks softly through the branches,
a dialect only the deeply attuned can decode;

it murmurs of storms passed, of gales imminent,
nature's breath: so wild, so rhythmed.
Seeds, potential tight in smallness,
await their turn to tap the dance of light;
　　their journey - a burst from the somber soil,
　　an ascent towards the endless blue canvas.

Forsaken Hymn no. 173

Open spaces stretch: the fields, the sky,
the universe: each breath, like his,
   held in the cradle of a star's blink.
Time's fabric, woven in the cosmic loom,
threads through my fingers, slipping,
as if to say, "All things pass."

Yet in the passage, the heart learns:
how foundations, seemingly solid, shift,
   how sorrow shapes the soul's geography,
changing contours, deepening valleys and
lifting eyes to new horizons:
   hope, a quiet ember, waits its turn to blaze.

Nearby, a river, loyal to its course,
reminds me: life is flow, not holding,
   wandering along paths of least resistance,
gathering memories, like fallen leaves,
   until all converges, the stream, the sea,
   and I find peace, at last, in continuity.

Forsaken Hymn no. 174

In the garden's grasp, chill whispers: cold,
   its breath, a mural of ice: each blade of grass
  a stroke from winter's paintbrush, stark, bold:
night's handiwork, the frost's delicate trespass.
Hoarfrost like thoughts on the cusp of bloom,
ribbons of ice spun from the loom of dark:
silence deep as the sky's high room,
vast as the stars: each spark a question mark.

  Stilled by the cold, the world turns slow,
ponderous, like the wheel of stars,
each leaf a print in the cosmos' show,
scripted in frost, bound by unseen scars.
Alone, I thread these icy paths,
footprints etched in the crystal mesh:
my breath a cloud, a whispering wraith,

haunting gardens where night and light thresh.
Nature's indifference—the unasked why
twines through each turn of earth's embrace:
in this chill, under the sigh
of stars, I seek warmth in the trace
of life: these patterns of frost and dew,
   a map of moments, paused, then gone:

Forsaken Hymn no. 175

In Archie's quiet echo, the symphony
of unplayed tunes, the missed connections:
life, with its relentless count, weaves
through us, thick with joys, woven with despairs,
each thread pulling taut, relaxing—
    a breath in the wind's hymn.

Under a child's airy rhyme, life moves
in chapters unclaimed by the loud voices—
    balancing the heavy prose with laughter,
light as scattered leaves, yet deep-rooted
      as the ancient oak: standing, waiting,
      bearing witness to the sky's broad arc.

And so we spin, each in our orbit, drawn
    by the grave tug of unseen moons, sharing
the quiet revolution of being, where every
silence is filled, every space thrums with stories—
    until the final line stretches out,
a gentle closing, a whispered goodnight.

Forsaken Hymn no. 176

Where river kisses ocean:
the tides mesh, serpentine,
sharp and sweet—life cycles
in the wash, salt weaves
through the warp and weft of sea,
quickening the earth:

think: all is interwoven:
paths of water, paths of air,
draped overhead like so much
celestial silk—molecules,
they swirl, seamless, in the gusts,
in the flights of gulls:

and what remains but to see
the pattern in the fray,
the design in the disarray:
    each end a thread pulled
from the loom's edge—taut, then
  released into the weave anew.

Forsaken Hymn no. 177

In the splay of evening light, here:
I stand, fringes of age and wisdom,
woven like a crown of laurel leaves,
each one a relic of battles fought,
softly: the decay and the bloom
  in cycles, as sure as moon tides.

Addison, my reflection, my rival,
your silhouette in the glass and gloam:
  how we mirror the complexities,
each pulse a notation in the grand score,
  our discordant harmony feeding
the roots of an ancient, gnarled oak.

Underneath the vast arch of sky,
where starlight sifts through the leaves,
  our hands, lined with the maps
of our years, reach out and falter,
then hold: the quiet truth of time
drawn close, in the whisper of twilight.

Forsaken Hymn no. 178

In the dance of shadows, substance shifts:
each leaf quivers under the weight
of its own dew-laden tale, whispering
of cycles: birth, bloom, wither, fall.
  But here I stand, listening,
as poplars narrate the sky.

The soil: a cradle of past lives;
roots entwine in a slow, silent ballet,
drawing from the depths, holding
  the earth's cold breath, warming it
with each exhalation: life's exchange
  in molecules and memories.

  What to make of this weave, complex
as the stories we hold close,
  or those we lose in the clutter
of daily surviving? How strange,
that in knowing, we fold and unfold
  into the earth, fulfilled.

Forsaken Hymn no. 179

In the hum of vast machinery, protocols:
 a chaos bound by rules unseen, where
particles dance on the edge of becoming,
unfolding like fern fronds at dawn: this
rip in the fabric of the mundane, a portal
to the whispered hymns of transformation.

The cosmos stretches, groaning with the weight
 of dark matter, unseen but felt: the gravity
of it all pulls at the corners of my mundane
thoughts, tethers them to the cold sweep of space
 where I find the lingering scent of stardust -
a reminder: all is in flux, nothing sits still.

And in this perpetuity, this endless reform,
 the turmoil seems less a battle than a ballet:
  forces in elegant disarray, crafting new worlds
from the old, a constant reimagining of what
is known; and so in stillness, amidst the fall
 of all else, I catch the grace of continuity.

Forsaken Hymn no. 180

Down by the frozen canals I linger:
each ice-glazed edge mirrors
the harshness of trials endured
in silence, under the weight of cold skies:
how nature binds with the body's shiver,
  like thoughts crystallized in mid-air.

Here, where Hart Crane once whispered
to the heedless wind, I hear
the hum of my own breath, a testament
  to survival, to the persistence
    of language and its infinite reach:
words floating over cold waters.

And in this unfolding scene, layers
reveal: the ice, a mere surface; beneath,
a river moves, unfettered and unseen,
    its currents mirroring our own depths
  ·of spirit and struggle: it flows,
bearing the weight of all our silent odes.

Forsaken Hymn no. 181

In this march of days, where shadows stretch:
   the firs stand tall, preaching in whispers
of survival, of stretching past dim limits
set by sky or soil, their green crowns
rustling a doctrine of diversity:
their truth, a simple complex of rising.

And below, the ground holds the seeds
   of revolt—each germ a potential titan
against the posture of ordained heights,
each leaf a testament to the wild's claim:
here, rights to light, to air, are taken—
   not given—by the assertive thrust of life.

What lessons, then, for us, nested in orders,
pondering the parity of our constructs?
Nature's court holds no bias to uniformity:
It celebrates the singular, the exceptional—
and so, in our quest for fairness, reckon
the beauty of bearing distinct skies.

Forsaken Hymn no. 182

In the dimming hum of nightfall's spree,
   sounds carry: light breezes, the call
of an owl: nature's embrace, closing
around the fizz and sputter of human joy,
  which like a river, finds its way:
through valleys of speech and peaks
of silence, cascading thoughts flow—
  translate the whispers of dark to dawn,

     interluding: the cosmos spins its quiet
philosophy through the weaving stars.
  How the mind stretches, an endless cosmos,
toward the dawn: eager for the light
to sculpt shadows into truths told
by the lingering echoes,
  repeating cycles of the moon's pull:

tides of thought, influx, retreat—
a dialogue with time, unending,
  bending around the orb of night,
each orbit a refrain of existence—
our stories, the universe conversing,
  whispering back to us, in stardust
and the first waking moments:

Forsaken Hymn no. 183

In the soft veins of leaves, chlorophyll:
sunlight trapped, bending towards the soil—
roots delve, heavy with earthly communion,
   where decay meets dawn: the cycle unmade.
   The murmurs of wind, a scientific hymn:
each breath an exchange: oxygen, carbon dioxide,
life's tender balance, calibrated

by unseen forces, the hidden laws
that govern the dance of dust and breath,
   light years told in the flap of a moth's wing.
Memory, too, weaves its webs in wetlands
of mind: neurons fire, pathways form,
the scent of old rain on pavement pulls
a childhood back from oblivion's brink.

Here, the past nests within the now—
   an echo persists, shaping each new day.
The process: continuous, unfailing,
like river currents carving canyons
deep into the crust of time, shedding layers,
   each stratum, a story buried, then exposed.

Forsaken Hymn no. 184

each reflection arises, morphs:
is it the mirror that lies, or merely
the angle of our gaze, shifting, elusive,
the way light bends at the horizon
or how water refracts the truth beneath?
a tree falls in the forest: sounds

   the same as dreams crumbling in silent depths—
nobody witnesses, yet the forest knows,
  records each echo in its ancient bark,
a testament to falls and growths unseen,
roots tangled in the earth's quiet hold.
we speak of time as if it's something held,

   not fluid, slipping through the clenched fists
  of our desires, shaping our hands
in its rushing: we are sculpted
as much by what we reach for
as by what we grasp: all things connected,
the cycle complete, each end tied to a beginning.

Forsaken Hymn no. 185

In the hum, my body a chart: decay plots
its course, each tooth a milestone, a marker
  of journey's wear: the grind, the inevitable set.
These tools of fine intrusion, probes and scrapers,
measure the depths, not just of enamel,
    but of time's pressing thumb.

How these moments thread through the eye
of a slender needle: pain, a bright line
drawn tight between past and future,
each tug a reminder: we are but soft
machinery, oiled, wearing down,
susceptible to the rust of years.

Yet, there is beauty in the breakdown,
flaws in the architecture singing
of battles fought, of seasons turned.
The cracks, where light gets in, where
growth sprouts from decay: so embracing
the end is but part of the process.

Forsaken Hymn no. 186

The spinning earth pauses: for a moment,
  shadows cast by this thinking, wondering
  soul: each thought a leaf falling, decaying
beneath the oak's wide, patient stance,
    humus enriching roots that grasp
deep, where worms interpret dark soils.

Energy flows where attention goes:
the photons dash from the sun,
collide with these open eyes
witnessing the ancient choreography
of light with leaf, breath with wind,
    life mingling with the inevitable tide.

In the span of a heartbeat: this universe,
    our brief echo in the immense silence,
  expands. Look: the stars weave us
into the night's dark fabric, seamlessly,
cradling the pulse of all our days,
holding close this shared dance, complete.

Forsaken Hymn no. 187

liberation to write undisturbed by the heartbeat of another
or a solitary confinement disguised, masking the void
   with eloquent phrases and metaphors for a moon alone:
    what links these souls to cosmos throbbing changes,
  each pulsar, each quasar, a lighthouse for wandering
thoughts, casting beams into the expanse of thought,

veins in the leaves trace patterns like neural pathways:
this interconnection: the root, the blossom, the decaying leaf:
does solitude nourish their minds or strip bare their bones
to their elemental truths, phosphorous and iron singing
within, the quiet hum of the universe whispering across
time: is the room devoid, or is it full of their silent echoes,

should we speak or listen as the dusk deepens, should we
   mourn their solitude or celebrate the unbound mind,
which like the river, carves canyons deep and wide,
  meandering, seeking, always returning to its source:
and so, in the quiet, understanding unfolds with the night,
clear as the stars that scribble ancient light across our sky.

Forsaken Hymn no. 188

The air hangs heavy with the scent of growth:
each fruit's blush, a testament to sun
and soil's dialogues, subtle, deep-rooted:
the chemistry of light, the physics of absorption.
Under these laden boughs, I thread through time,
entangled in memories as branches in the wind.

In the gentle sway, her laughter echoes—
a melody carried over seasons, and I
am adrift in the orchard's arms, caught
between the fading light and the first stars:
   how the mind, too, grafts new shoots
from old wood, reaching for light in shadow's breath.

Here, where past and present mingle like roots,
   each leaf a syllable in nature's persistent whisper,
I find the constants, like gravity, like love,
  guiding the unseen courses of our lives.
In this quiet communion, beneath the infinite,
   all things fold back into the earth, completed.

Forsaken Hymn no. 189

Beneath the silent eaves, snow whispers:
   deep secrets painting, a white hush pauses.
  The world listens: my heart counts the absent,
miles to Iowa stretch, cold under snow's damp touch.
Alone, I navigate silence, wide and yawning,
rooms echo with the ghosts of laughter gone.

My dog, companion in quiet, understands
   neither distance nor the span of time delayed,
but sits by, loyalty a warmth unfailing.
The car rests, frozen, stubborn under white,
   as if to say some stops we choose and some
are chosen for us: all is still, deeply still.

  Persistence in gentle flakes, layering softly:
everywhere traces new beginnings or erasures.
Together, apart, enveloped in frost's breath,
the essence of presence dances, intricate,
across whispering, frozen landscapes:
here in this quiet, all converging thoughts find rest.

Forsaken Hymn no. 190

Under the boughs, I pause: my thoughts
adorned with the rustle of old leaves,
echoing long-lost poets' dreams,
wrestling with time's unyielding tide,
where each wrinkle in the bark
mirrors one upon my own skin.

The soil, heavy with past rains:
a testament to cycles unbroken,
feeding the roots, drawing from decay
the potent promise of renewal—
each seed stirring beneath the winter's
ghost, poised for the spring's warm whisper.

What solace, then, in the green returning,
in the knowledge that what fades feeds
the forthcoming? The finite dance
of leaves, once vibrant, now returning to earth
to mingle with forgotten songs:
in endings, the echo of beginnings.

Forsaken Hymn no. 191

In the cool dusk, leaves: a panoply:
amber and crimson, falling,
    each descent tracing arcs of being—
brief etchings against the sky's vast canvas:
this autumn bereaves its glory,
yielding to winter's imminent claim.
My wife, with stern grace,

handles the mortality of insects,
each act a small, ordained fall—
not unlike leaves, or fading light,
or the bird that met its end:
an echo in the weave of predation.
As Archie mourns, I ponder:
life's stark frame, the intertwine

of joy, grief—each leaf a symbol
of what we gain and lose and never hold.
Here, in this seasonal shedding,
I grasp the fragile thread of continuity.
In the chill air, each breath visible,
a reminder of the warmth that life insists.

Forsaken Hymn no. 192

continual echo: a reminder from those who
once stood by our side, shaping
our hearts through their absence
and presence alike: But how does one
retain the whispers?
Every leaf that falls speaks to change:
   it decays, feeding the earth, calling

us to accept the cycles
that bind: the living, the dead, intermixed
in perpetuity: And so, love adapts,
its roots deep, entwined in the fertile
   soil of past lessons.
We stretch towards the sun, our days filled

   with striving and rest, discovering
that to grow is not just to ascend
but also to reach out: to connect:
   where horizons of understanding and
forgiveness intersect, becoming our
   clear sky, our calm.

Forsaken Hymn no. 193

In dim shadows, life's frail seams stretch:
  the fine line between vigor and decline,
    echoed in a friend's strained whisper:
throat raw, body caught like prey
  in the relentless teeth of the temporal
we lie, thoughts tangled in bedsheets:
abiding the twining of decay with life,

  how delicate our existence,
how easily unraveled by the smallest tear,
the least fray in our corporeal fabric
philosophers ponder, yet cells break
day by day: entropy's quiet crescendo:
yet in this surrender, a peculiar peace,
yielding not to dark, but to the dawning

  of understanding: in our end, the whole
sum of us, softly rendered complete.
  Shadows play: they steep the walls,
drift like thoughts on the edge of sleep,
where the boundary of flesh and time thins,
each pulse a soft drum, the rhythm of life
slowly syncing with the whisper of decay:

Forsaken Hymn no. 194

where the wind begins: I cannot see
    its birthing place, only the leaves
hurried along like worshippers
swept into the fold, their whispers
a creed recited in rustles,
the high branches bending in faith.

I tread the damp earth, its soft crust
yielding beneath my weight: a sign
of unseen life below, the dark
    soil's slow, tireless processes
transforming death back to life, broad
spectrum cycles in miniature.

And yet, in this moment of flux,
where all things converse in the dance
  of growth and decay, I stand still,
    anchored by the gift of breathing,
knowing I too am a brief part
of an unending conversation.

Forsaken Hymn no. 195

In the seminar's quiet hum, I excavate:
   fossils of thoughts, each layer
  compressed by the weight of years,
  organic matter transformed
  into relics, dense with the sudden
spark of connecting old and new.

The chalkboard holds equations—
the calculus of human spirit
   intersecting with the unknown:
how a heart weighs the sum
  of its breaches and mendings,
   the residue of each calculation.

Here, in this gathering of minds,
we parse the syntax of our souls,
unraveling the helix of legacy
to find the basal thread:
our shared lineage in the stardust,
precisely charted, yet ever expansive.

Forsaken Hymn no. 196

In the quiet room where thoughts collide,
    the windowed light casts shadows long:
each a farewell, a soft dissent
against the curtain of the coming dark.
A leaf, in its descent, knows the twist
of wind, the inevitability of soil:
firm in its place in the turn of seasons,

each parting a prelude to a return.
  Glasses forgotten, catch fleeting light,
    briefly hold the sun's last declining rays:
in them, the universe's grandeur
reduced to the sparkle of an instant.
  The headlines fade, as all must,
words that once screamed importance

    now whisper in the corners of attics,
dust-laden, the ink still proud but unseen.
And so, we chase knowledge, as if
to pin down the fleeting butterfly of truth:
but in the net, the colors blur—
we find not the captured, but the changed.

Forsaken Hymn no. 197

Veins of silver moonlight: the earth
  knows itself as it shifts, breathes,
  its whispers crawling through the dew-soaked
grass: each blade a story in silhouette.
  The landscape melds: memories, the soft
crush of past footfalls in fertile soil,
  a communion of roots and decay: life cycles,

  woven beneath the ever-watchful gaze
of constellations: the stellar cartographers
  charting our impermanence.
This continuous thread, pulled tight by gravity,
  draws the arc of a hawk: precision in dive,
  the same force that clutches at the apple,
  ripe, inevitably yielding to the ground:

  how everything returns, a testament
  to cycles that bind atom to orbit.
  Through layers of night, the echoes of those
  who came before us tread lightly on the edge
  of our consciousness, flickering in the peripheral
vision: a reminder of our transient stride
  across timelines, vast and unfathomable.

Forsaken Hymn no. 198

In the crisp morning where dew meets dawn,
the earth speaks in whispers: how each blade of grass
holds a droplet, a world of its own: microcosms
reflecting the infinite stretch of sky—here is
the smallness of existence, punctuated by sunlight,
    and there, the vastness.

    Interlaced: roots and soil, neuron and synapse:
  each a network: detailed and vast.
    The flowers tilt toward the light, phototropic,
  each movement a gentle arc, a leaning into
life's embrace, the physics of survival
meshed with the aesthetic of desire.

From petal to bone, leaf to thought, all connected,
this body of mine, prone yet awake, senses
a companionship with the world's turning:
cycles: seasons charting time, growth,
and inevitable decay.
And so, in the quiet acknowledgment, we are whole.

Forsaken Hymn no. 199

Through the scope of day: each morning
reveals its schism, as if light splits
not just clouds but continents of thought,
and shadows that once danced along
the edges now loom, large and brooding,
   over fields grown wild with neglect.

Yet, there, by the roadside: an old car,
  windowless, rust-ridden, bares its ribs
like a carcass. Nature: reclaiming
what we discard, the chassis softens
under moss, gears give way to ivy,
the engine silent, entwined in vines.

  A reminder: all comes, and goes too,
   even the darkest cloud breaks to blue,
even iron returns to the soil
   from which it came, and strife finds solace
in the arms of the inexorable
cycle: decay breathes life anew.

Forsaken Hymn no. 200

Across the street, light dances on glass:
courthouse windows reflecting more than
   the mere façade of law and order: freedom,
slyly woven through the threads of human fates,
negotiated in whispers, sealed with a nod.
   The war of words, between bites of cold,
a spectacle of suited soldiers, their briefcases

not as burdensome as the souls they carry,
or scatter lightly like ashes on icy sidewalks,
where every step might slip on unsaid deals.
A limousine cuts through the chill, sleek and
   unrelenting, as if to mock the biting breeze—
Christmas whispers promises, forgotten yet
flickering like a candle in the wind:

a dream's tribute beneath the burdened boughs.
The river of law rushes on, swollen and swift,
indifferent to the plea of peace this cold season.
The snow-blanketed park offers itself, palliative
to all souls passing by: a silent, snowy comfort,
a canvas white with the cold truths of justice.

Forsaken Hymn no. 201

    Under the fading glow, thoughts drip:
    like rainwater, seeping through the cracks,
finding their slow course: how the earth
    shifts, minutely, under weight unseen,
nourished by a storm's still hush,
the silence left behind the roar.

My mind weaves between the lines
of heavy books: those ancient woods
    dense with the musk of ink and time;
    each step taken sinks, slightly, into
a loam rich with decayed wisdom,
    the path branching endlessly forward.

In this dimming embrace, I eye
the murky limits of my sagging shelf:
its burden not just leather-bound,
but the heft of being, fluid and flux,
each day's close a soft seal on night:
    the perfect pause to ponder stars.

Forsaken Hymn no. 202

In the sterile gleam of fluorescent tubes,
the hums and beeps that orchestrate our pulse:
    life swings, a pendulum between echoes
    of sterile whispers and the loud silence
    that inhabits the night's long, astringent watch.
Each breath a note in the symphony of survival.

Tangles of wires, like vines, climb across flesh,
charting paths of soft tissue and hard bone—
mysterious landscapes under thin gauze.
Hands, sterile, reaching out in routine care
yet hold the warmth of a shared human plight:
    the firm grip of grappling with mortality.

In this choreography of quiet battles,
    each step weaves through corridors of resolve,
past walls bearing the scars of countless souls.
Beneath the clinical light, spirits rise,
the unseen dance of atoms and affections:
thus, in healing, we find our truest selves.

Forsaken Hymn no. 203

In the whisper of late night clicks,
the hum of screens: Is this connection?
   Devices chatter, the world contracts,
    seeping through circuits,
     small talk amplified through wires,
our voices boxed in digital echoes.

Is there still space for silence,
    a solitude untouched by gaze?
Through windows, distant laughter rises,
a bird's shadow crosses the moon,
and yet, here, between calls,
    solitude is a screen, flickering.

Each pulse of light, every ring,
binds me to a web, sprawling wide:
we spin threads, invisible, tight,
linking not just lands but minds.
Yet, amidst this relentless tide,
    silence waits, beyond reach, complete.

Forsaken Hymn no. 204

In this dim chamber, notes collide
like photons in the stark expanse:
   each key a universe, echoing
      past the confines of black and white.
    The metronome ticks—a soft pulse
that marries time with the infinite.

Rilke's whispers slide along the ivory,
   thin cries tethered to the gravity of sound.
My fingers press down: laws disintegrate,
   music spilling over the edge of order,
where structure meets the unmeasured
breaths of those lost to the ocean's keep.

Each chord is a wave rolling back to sea,
reclaiming what was never ours to hold.
Here, with Beethoven's shadow, I find
   the tempestuous peace of unresolved melodies.
In the hum of strings, a gentle closure:
   each ending note a beginning anew.

Forsaken Hymn no. 205

In the shaded room where silence wrings:
a symphony in each dusty corner,
softly, the twilight deepens, stretches,
its cool fingers tracing the spines of books,
hum of evening thickening, the air
ripe with the scent of forgotten lore.

  Outside, stars blink into existence:
  indifferent, distant, yet deeply courted
  by the eyes of him who stood alone,
  crafted constellations in his mind,
    worlds where youth fades, relentless, quick—
a harsh whisper in the vast dark.

  Inside, I linger by the window frame,
contemplating the dance of leaves,
ephemeral yet eternal, swaying,
a testament to the cycle: birth and return.
All of life, a fleeting verse:
    finally, a quiet understanding of peace.

Forsaken Hymn no. 206

In the hush of old stones and echo:
thought—threadbare yet persistent—
    weaves through the mortar, finding
cracks where light insists
on entry: here, the mindful pausing,
discourse with the dust
of books, their spines aligning like vertebrae:

    a backbone of knowledge held upright
by the quiet defiance of men
whose brilliance formed not in applause
  but in the shadows they chose
to cultivate: such fertile solitude.
Amid this garden of stone and tome,

    ideas uncurl like leaves in spring,
timeworn yet anew. How easily
the mind contends with contradictions—
    each conclusion a node in the vast
network of unending inquiry.
In seeking, we honor their paths:

Forsaken Hymn no. 207

Beneath the thin ice: molecules
writhe in their unseen ballet:
   connections forge and break, where
touch is more than touch, and
   speech, less than molecules exchanged.
The roots delve deep, far below
the sun's gentle probe: silent
in dark earth, they mingle, strive,

yield, and thrive: a network
   of unseen strength: feeding, holding.
So are we, linked beneath our casual
hello, goodbye: atoms in
perpetual negotiation: the oak
   stands firm, knowing its leaves
are destined to depart, yet

it thrives: as do we, rooted in unseen depths.
In the quiet respite of dusk:
leaves murmur secrets,
   as if each drop of twilight knows
the hidden cadences of wind,
teaching barren branches how
to hold the weight of snow.

Forsaken Hymn no. 208

Leaves twist down: a slow gyre,
  autumn stripping its canvas,
bare edges where life recedes
yet, by this window, thoughts
flutter: a letter's weight in hand,
echoing the pulse of distant bonds.

  Shifts in the wind—like voices
  in the literary spread on my desk:
Middle Eastern poets weave
through Western critique, layers
of insights, some dried like fields
  after harvest, demanding renewal.

And so, amid these intersections
  of thought and legacy, my family
merges like streams, complex,
reflective: my sister's laughter,
a bright splash on water's face,
ending, for now, in the calm of home.

Forsaken Hymn no. 209

Each step forward: an insistence,
a whisper against harsh silence,
defying the white: stark, unyielding.
   The universe coolly debates my presence,
my claims laid out with every tread:
   discursive footnotes in snow.

Yet, the deeper dialogue: muffled
by the crunch beneath, where tiny crystals
mirror vast stars—cold distant, twinkling.
How determinate, these patterns of ice:
structured, yet blindly sculpted
by winds that never face denial.

I laugh, breath hanging like a cloud,
firm in my path, while around me,
   continents of snow shift—imperceptibly.
This landscape: both map and territory,
   where every breaking step, a note
in the quiet symphony of persistence.

Forsaken Hymn no. 210

In this stretch of boardwalk, wood worn
by countless soles: echoes resonate,
each grain preserving whistles,
the soft shuffle of steps sequestered
   in winter's harsh embrace: here, the silence
speaks louder than the summer's roar.

Amid the echoes, a soliloquy unfolds,
   whispers carried on briny breezes:
the slot machines lie dormant, their bright
    lights dimmed, a juxtaposition—
once symbols of vibrant chance, now
   silent sentries in the off-season's chill.

This space, molded by human hands yet
abandoned, becomes sanctified by absence,
each empty bench, a pew; the ferris wheel,
a slow-turning altar against the gray sky.
I find myself walking, seeking not divine
but the divine in the mundane—complete.

Forsaken Hymn no. 211

Beneath my fingers: landscapes drawn
in clicks and clacks: mountains rise,
   valleys fold: whispers of distant myth
echo through typewritten trails;
the keys, like footsteps, chart paths
never walked, yet deeply known.

In this quiet study, the world's edge
blurs: my thoughts, swathed in paper,
meet seas not sailed: the ink,
a vessel for voyages unnumbered,
flows like a river: carving canyons
   in the white expanse of untouched pages.

Each letter a footprint in soft earth,
bridging the gap: from mind to matter:
where thoughts ferment like dark ouzo,
a silent symphony in the solitude.
   Here, at journey's end, the keys rest,
and I find peace in the promise of pages turned.

Forsaken Hymn no. 212

    deep consciousness, where atoms indulge
their merry dance around the void's inheritance:
  nuclei claiming their spots: the dance of space
tight with energy, bursting through the seams
of reality, so finely woven by the threads
  of quantum leaps and philosophical dreams.

  A leaf, mid-air, pirouettes on the whim
of a sudden gust: it knows not despair,
nor does it question the wind's motive
  or the tree's silent approval of its flight:
here, a lesson, not in physics alone but in
the surrender to the circuits of existence.

For who among us can claim dominion
over the myriad paths the universe
    decides to carve? Our thoughts,
  like rivers, cut through the terrain of days,
resolute yet ever adapting to the land;
in the end, composing a story that holds.

Forsaken Hymn no. 213

Under the indecisive sky, spring hesitates:
each branch outlined in the sharp breath
of a season waking, slow,
uncertain if it mourns or celebrates:
frost's retreat marked by the muddy scars
that map the path of thawing.
 Nature's indifferent to our cluttered lives,
  circling back, always, to subtle conquer:

roots probing, shoots breaking through
  what remains of winter's armor:
 the sun stretches longer,
  casting shadows where snow once whispered
  its cold wisdom about impermanence.
 We stumble, often, on these soft edges,
  the boundary blurring between broken

and burgeoning anew:
  where Archie's steps meet my own,
failures composed with the rhythm of seasons,
  our missteps, another layer
in the sediment of stories,
  the earth absorbing each fall,
unjudging, ever turning.

Forsaken Hymn no. 214

In the quiet: a leaf falls, a decision:
to surrender, charting descent
through still air, each turn a testament
to gravity's unfailing pull: how it calls
every atom back to the embrace of earth:
this is the nature of things, inherent:
   the rise must bow to fall, and in between,

the holding: the breath, the pause, the unseen
effort to stay aloft: all life is spent
in the balance of hanging and dropping:
and so we find ourselves, subjects under
   the vast canopy of wondering stars,
bound by the same rules that govern the scars
   left by meteors: within, the thunder

of heartbeat, echoing universe's whisper:
all returns, all renews, in the quieter closure.
In the whisper of wind through winter twigs,
the region of frost has shaped its hold:
each branch a notation, crisp and bold,
on nature's vast, unfolding score.

Forsaken Hymn no. 215

Within these walls: old books, a whisper of dust,
the fine echo of time's eloquent crust:
  Yeats stirs the quiet with his silver cane,
  each tap a drumbeat, all rhythms sustain
the dance of ideas, where brilliance meanders,
broad strokes of genius: context expands us.

The tendrils of steam from the teapot to air,
a ballet of mist, faintly seen, barely there,
like thoughts half-formed, waiting to condense
into clarity, into witty recompense,
where history's weight seems a feather, light,
  balanced on the fulcrum of deep insight.

This time, this space, a suspension of sorts,
where present encounters the past's retorts,
our discourse floating, a leaf on a stream,
drifting toward some forgotten dream;
in this convergence, eternity's breath—
    our moment's mark on the doorstep of death.

Forsaken Hymn no. 216

In malls, light flickers off polished surfaces:
gloss and sheen promising more than they hold.
Every echo shaped by commerce,
yet beneath, a stillness, a question:
how filled are these young hearts that wander
    aisles stacked like the years they've yet to live?

I hear laughter, sharp and digital,
clips of joy, truncated by the next distraction.
Screens glow, casting pale light on faces
searching for the next delight, the next pulse
    of ephemeral contentment—
a hunger, never knowing it's hungry.

In their eyes, the reflection of a world
vast and intricate, reduced to pixels and sound bytes.
Yet, can these souls sift through the chaff,
    find roots in this shifting, sanded landscape?
This generation, inheriting the wind—
may they learn to breathe, deeply, the fragrant earth.

Forsaken Hymn no. 217

In this quiet room, light sifts through:
dust motes dance, something celestial
in their random paths that mirror
the random steps of nations, drawn, redrawn,
boundaries marked and obliterated like
history's footnotes fading in the dawn.

    Every whisper here breathes stories of loss—
the sharp inhale of Cold Harbor's shadows,
Korean hills, or Bay of Pigs, their echoes
fade in the volumes of collective memory:
each name a whisper growing fainter
with the turning pages of time.

Yet these walls, these books, inquire deeply
    into what we remember: why some sorrows
lodge so firmly in the heart's chamber
while others slip through, like sand
through fingers, lost in the vast sieve
of what is cherished, what forgotten.

Forsaken Hymn no. 218

In the marrow of the leaf: each vein,
  a map to the sun: photosynthesis:
a light caught between the spaces
where shadows shift, signaling change,
  compressing time between a sigh
and the vast silence that follows.

Change clasps the pulse of earth:
roots twine, unwind, in moist communion:
  soil, rich with the decay of fallen titans,
recycles vitality with each season's turn,
where buried seeds awaken, stretch,
    and thrust toward the urgency of light.

Through these cycles, I find the cadence
of breath, pauses heavy with thought:
the sky arches, a continuous bridge
connecting moments like stars-
  a constellation of remembered whispers:
here I stand, whole, at the edge of rebirth.

Forsaken Hymn no. 219

Brushed by winds of profound dialogue,
the crow: wings spanning rifts of silence,
drifts on thermal philosophies: high,
   higher, where thoughts condense—
turn liquid, nearly solid: almost touchable.
  Murmurs in twilight, thread through trees,
    each leaf a syllable, a flickering shadow
on the manuscript of earth. Here,

nature scripts in seamless flux:
mutations penned in chlorophyll—
the page turns with a gust.
  In these vibrations, a resonance:
a crow's call across the expanse of becoming.
Soaring, it unbinds the dense narrative,
our understanding ripening in the fall air,

each moment a ferment, until
  all resolves into the quiet closure of dusk.
In the half-light, thoughts meld:
particle to wave, silence
to murmur: a crow's flight
  charts the invisible, rides the unseen
  drafts stitched between the cool threads of air.

Forsaken Hymn no. 220

beneath the skin of the world, roots twist:
    a network of synapses firing dark signals
    through loam, each thread a silent call
to commune, to bind high leaf to buried node:
water travels where gravity suggests, slow
and persistent, shaping stone, whispering through
    canyon walls: listen, it says, to the pulse of sediment,

to the erosion of time that reveals, that teaches:
ideas, like rivers, carve landscapes in the mind,
meandering paths that loop and return,
the erosion of certainty, the sedimentation of thought:
how each drop of knowing alters the whole,
    how we, standing at the confluence of past

and possibility, feel the rush of colder waters,
  the merge: here, I grasp the fleeting edge
of insight, where understanding blooms
in the quiet aftermath of the river's roar,
in the calm clarity of pooled waters,
reflecting sky, clouds, and the flight of birds:

Forsaken Hymn no. 221

Change, the recurrent whisper:
  how it shapes the curve of hills,
edges worn by persistent winds,
    or the slow river that carves its bed:
endless, yet each moment sealed,
unique within its shifting sands.

Life clings, tendrils sprouting from cracks:
resilient in its audacious stretch
    towards the sun, its daily resurrection.
Decay juxtaposes birth in seamless cycles:
  leaves composting as they enrich the soil,
feed the roots that uphold our standing.

Under the starless cloak of night,
my thoughts spiral like autumn leaves,
searching for where decay aligns with birth,
each end knotted firmly to a beginning.
Amid these endless transformations,
the stillest hour arrives, complete.

Forsaken Hymn no. 222

In the fading light, thoughts unfurl:
how closely twined, the innocent sprout
and the strangling vine: this dance
    where shadows play both shield and shroud:
our nature's tightrope walk between
birth's bloom and the decay it rounds.

Actions, like seeds cast on the wind,
find places to root, in light or dank:
the golden glow's shadow stretches,
    elongated tales that sway our sight,
pointing, always, to the just or unjust,
yet, who cultivates the judge's bench?

This breathing earth cycles through
    its green pulse and fallow rest:
here, a melon, lush in its hidden sweet,
there, a barren patch, soil spent and grieving:
we, gardeners of chance and choice,
tend each plot, await what truth the harvest brings.

Forsaken Hymn no. 223

    Morning shifts: light slices through leaves,
angles steep, sharp as a cat's leap: grace
in thin contours, like innocence slipping
through fingers that grasp, thinking, always,
at the manner of burdens, the why of weight:
who decides the heaviness of hearts?

  Sparrows chirp the queries of existence,
from wire to wire: a coded song,
each note a drop, each drop an echo,
resonating in the chambers of thought.
Midday's sun weighs down, pressing
    questions into the shadows, my mind a maze.

    As the sun arcs, thoughts trail:
    each question a thread, unspooled,
mapping the dance of light and darkness,
shadowplay on mundane surfaces,
where understanding meets the brink,
and silence, golden, fills the spaces left.

Forsaken Hymn no. 224

In the abbey's shadow, echoes cling:
hymns reverberate through cold stone halls,
worn smooth by time's relentless turning,
    where light dwindles into corners, grave and still.
Outside, the burning cane leans at his side:
a signet of survival, its deep scars etched
    by seasons harsh and harvests failed,
marking lines as on the oldest trees

where bark splits, revealing histories
layered in the map of years it stood.
Inside this heart, corridors run deep,
memories like tapestries, frayed but held
taut by the weave of ongoing thought.
Here we stand together, sifting through
what remains, finding beauty

in the disintegration, as much as in the vigor.
    The silence now speaks as loudly
    as any word we once declared in youth,
the mind sharpens on the edge
of the abyss: time's precipice calls us
to join the past with the present,
and in this merging, find peace.

Forsaken Hymn no. 225

I wander through the mind's twisted corridors
under a moon, tinged with the hues of madness:
and the stark clarity of sobriety, pondering
the old adage, how roots link underground,
    silent: yet a network bustling with whispers,
each fiber stretching towards another's echo.

Through the soil's dense layers, particles shift,
each grain: a cosmos of atoms in restless dance,
bound by forces unseen, yet palpable as the wind
    that charts its unseen paths through forest canopies,
where leaves flutter, each a small sail: tugged
at the whim of breaths that speak in gusts.

And so, we find the nature of change: inevitable,
woven into the fabric of existence like decay
in fallen logs, or the slow melt of glaciers that
    reshape landscapes, silently insisting on renewal.
All converges in the cycle, the pulse rhythmically
sustaining: all life connected, coming back to dust.

Forsaken Hymn no. 226

In the midst of tumult, where echos collide:
her hair swathes like curtains in gust-driven rain,
tangles of wetness, a shroud, and a shade—
each strand a filament charged with surviving,
   the turmoil a backdrop for delicate strength,
interwoven like roots beneath us.

Thunder reverberates, a pulsing heart;
animal eyes wide, the shared pulse of fear:
they know the storm, as do I, its cruel rhythm,
where surprisingly tender green shoots can emerge
   from the soil of disaster: so, love, too, might grow—
twisting skyward, resilient and raw.

Her silhouette, faint amidst the haze,
suggests the contours of hope, defining
a space where despair might yet yield to creation;
   in her presence: a manuscript of the possible,
authored by the quiet intersections of heartbeats,
   ending: in our shared embrace of the storm.

\

Forsaken Hymn no. 227

Moonlight fractures through the blinds:
   each sliver a shard of memory,
     fragmented yet sharp, piercing
the fabric of the now: they twirl,
specters caught in the gravity
of past orbits, relentless in their path.

    These papers: cast-offs, strewn,
  the detritus of fevered thoughts
   and lost conversations: where does
the space between words widen
   into a canyon of silence,
   a lacuna bridging thought with loss?

My mother's frozen smile,
stern yet tender in the silver glow,
implores a rethinking: what bounds
set us apart, yet under the same sky
we breathe, weave, live—
all ties return to their beginnings.

Forsaken Hymn no. 228

The mill wheel turns: erosion,
the slow dance of water on stone,
   declaring the might of gentle forces
  that shape without possession:
each groan a testament to time's sway,
each splash a note in nature's symphony.

This flume—nature's vein—pulses,
feeds the earth, whispers secrets
   of birth and decay, cycles spun
from the loom of the seasons:
  how the trout swims upstream,
  a spectacle of effort against the flow.

And we, spectators on the bank,
mistake the dance as ours to lead,
   forgetting the river choreographs
each step with ancient rhythms:
in its mirror, the sky bends, touches tips
with reeds in the quiet conclusion of day.

Forsaken Hymn no. 229

a whisper of carbon whispers: old stones
breathing deep, eternal circulations
of water, leaf by leaf: the ceaseless tasks
of breaking down and building up: fractals
    of existence timed, not by clocks but by
  slow grips of root in crumbling soil:

each drop of rain: a pulse in the vast
vein of atmospheres: cycles spinning
out of the throb of earth's molten heart:
microcosms in every splash that splits
    against the pavement, where city meets
the tempest's dance, a blend of grey and green:

so the ancient hands guide, not to heights
    beyond our breathing, but deeper in:
  into the humus-rich black that feeds
each new seed: thus, under these skies, I learn:
    to grow is not to escape but to return,
  to the beginning, where all is one.

Forsaken Hymn no. 230

Across the valley, shadows lengthen:
the sun slips behind cloaked hills,
    but light lingers, playing on edges
of leaves, tracing the subtle veins
like roads on a weathered map—
paths traced, retraced by wandering gusts.

  In the dwindling twilight, truths
seem clearer, as if daylight
tangles thoughts with its bright threads.
How easily we lose the thread
    in the gold glare of noon:
but as shadows merge, so do meanings.

Words once light as leaves,
when whispered at dusk, gain weight,
settle in the space between us
  like stones warming with residual sun.
Here, in the closing of day,
    all is connected, all roles fulfilled.

Forsaken Hymn no. 231

Across the room, the shadows play:
grace notes to the dimming day,
softness seeping through the cracks
of the dome where light lacks,
spilling ink on Archie's tale:
his whiskers, a silent, fallen flail.

The curve of his spine a silent arch,
a bridge from light to the encroaching dark;
    each vertebra a story told,
in the shrinking light, grown cold.
Nature's manuscript, ever cruel,
penalties paid by no clear rule.

Yet, in this flux of fade and sigh,
    where the boundaries of being lie,
there's a dance of atoms, wild, serene,
    whispering of what might have been:
And so, in the calm that dusk affords,
we find our truths, our words restored.

Forsaken Hymn no. 232

In the hush of evening's dip, photons
   scatter into twilight: they weave through leaves,
   each leaf a stipple on the vast canvas
of day's surrender: nature's precise breaths
   dictate the pace of decay: the slow turn
from green vigor to the gold of spent youth.

   Quantum flutters, the unseen forces pull:
atoms dance in the ambiguous light,
every moment a collision of past
with possibility: this tender balance
   between becoming and unbecoming,
mirroring our own perpetual sway.

   Thus, we find in the scatter of stars,
the pattern of our own resolve: the push
to extract from the marrow of each night
the kernel of dawn: here, in the cool wash
of infinity, our questions rest,
settled, as the universe whispers home.

Forsaken Hymn no. 233

In the wake of rainfall: nature's sigh
rinses the slate, leaves a shine on the leaf,
a gloss in the eye: the world under a fresh light
where droplets cling to twigs, suspended,
in the delicate balance of gravity and surface tension:
each a microcosm, reflecting whole universes.

Thunder—resonates, a low rumble from afar,
echoing decisions, the paths chosen or left behind:
a fish instincts its route to ancient spawning grounds
as bats trace their silent, sonar-guided arcs through dusk,
navigating by echoes we can hardly imagine,
coding space in the language of echoes.

Yet here I stand, human, all too human,
grappling with the gossamer threads of understanding,
where each interaction is both light and shadow:
the complexities of connection, like water slipping
through the spaces between fingers,
and in the trickling remnants, truths echo clear.

Forsaken Hymn no. 234

In the shed's calm, the world contracts:
splinters, a testament to labor's call,
  and dust spins in the beam, particles
aligning in the light like stars in faint
nebulas: each shaving a galaxy, each
  echo a profound expanse of time.

Here, where hands shaped fate
from wood's resistance, I seek:
principles that bind as tightly as the
grain that runs deep beneath the stain—
change shaped by love, simplicity,
from the carpenter's rough palms.

In this quiet craft of living, what
foundations we lay in silent acts,
how we turn the wheel, chisel
  at the block of our own stubbornness,
  seek truths in simple shavings, and
at last, align with enduring paths.

Forsaken Hymn no. 235

Amid the lore of fallen leaves: the cycle,
inexorable, whispers rust-browned truths,
the earth's soft claim: decay feeds new blooms,
reciprocity in roots and decay;
yet here, Hemingway's shade murmurs:
    in every pen's stroke, the potential for undoing;
    a father's legacy: shelter or shadow—

how finely a line divides protect from smother.
In the knitting of veins on fallen leaves,
the structure speaks: the same pathways
that channel life can strangle and restrain,
threads of existence bound in tight weaves—
hope and despair, the twin pulse felt beneath
    the weight of history's unsteady hand,

each moment, every choice: brushstrokes
on the canvas of continuance, the art of surviving;
so, in this haunted twilight, this soft bending
of light through old windows, one contemplates
the architecture of the self amid time's relics,
the spirit seeking balance between creation's joy
    and the quieter, darker side of legacy.

Forsaken Hymn no. 236

Leaf by leaf, the square fills: nature's script
unfolding in human forms, each body a node
   in a vast network: how easily they sway,
caught in the gentle pulse of spring winds.
Yet, in this dance of light and shadow,
I see the balancing scales: each action a weight.

   Crisp air cuts through the fabric of morning,
     beneath a sky so wide, so achingly blue,
   it mocks the smallness of our concerns:
   here, at the junction of earth and ether,
where truths are whispered by the rustling
     leaves, each whisper a verdict on our deeds.

   These are the moments we gather, hold tight,
as if by holding we might shift the balance,
tilting towards a less burdened future:
the crowd disperses: the square empties,
   leaving only the echo of footsteps, and
     the justice of a quiet morning settles in.

Forsaken Hymn no. 237

Beneath the crab-apple tree's gnarled grasp,
the air thick with the musk of spilled secrets,
roots delve deep, threading through earth's dark tapestry:
each fiber a silent witness to human follies,
absorbing whispers like water from soil,
  fusing leaf, limb, life, and legacies.

Light slices through branches: sharp, precise—
a scalpel revealing the anatomy of night.
  Here, amid delicate dances of shadow and regret,
the tree stands sentinel over transient hearts,
its bark scarred by the ceaseless scroll of seasons,
    years etched like scientific names in a ledger.

  In this quiet aftermath, contemplation blooms:
how intimately bound, the cycle of growth and decay,
nature's indifferent rhythms chart courses of change,
the finality: a tree felled, lovers lost, tales ended.
  Yet, from decay springs new life, roots reaching,
in the hush that follows, whispers of new beginnings.

Forsaken Hymn no. 238

Amid the speckled dark, constellations wheel:
each star, a note in a grand cosmic score,
orchestrated without conductor, where
chaos dances with precision: such mystery
    is the mere inkling of divine jest,
or perhaps, an experiment in freedom.

In the cradle of such vastness, my desk
spills over with scripts of human concerns—
    papers that whisper of time, eroding like stone
a testament to the fleeting beats
    of our hearts: quick, quick, slow—
each pulse a stammer against eternity.

So, what of this clutter? Each item, a relic
of a day's urgent yet transient striving.
    Through the window, the universe laughs gently,
offering neither rebuke nor redemption, but
a simple reminder: in the immense weave of it all,
even chaos molds new worlds from the shadows.

Forsaken Hymn no. 239

At the fringe of day, twilight:
when starlight winks on, each
    flicker a whisper, tentative,
as if questions could be
stars—each a burning pivot
    of doubt and dazzle:

    the mind, too, orbits mysteries,
    turns on the dark matter
of contemplation, bending around
thought's gravity: what casts
me in shadow, casts me
also in light:

in silence, vast as cosmos,
the heart balances on the scale
of past and possible, weighs
each act, each intention,
as if to divine, in the stretch
of unspoken spaces, closure.

Forsaken Hymn no. 240

Under the dome of space: wood creaks,
time swells like the lungs of the hall,
  breathing in the dust of graphite,
out: the sigh of soft erasures.
Pages turn, a quiet whisper against
the clatter of minds unfolding:
each answer a branch that reaches
for the light of understanding,

yet shadows itself in doubt:
  the nature of human endeavor.
Seasons cycle through windowpanes,
leaves pressed against glass, observed
like specimens pinned in stillness:
  each leaf: a lesson in letting go.
Chalk dust settles on the floor:

a thin film, a galaxy slowly forming
beneath the soles of shoes restless
  to leave, yet bound to this orbit.
Here, where thought circles back,
I find peace amid the stretch
and contract: the in and out breath
  of knowledge: a lungful of sky.

Forsaken Hymn no. 241

the world, old beyond counting, still pulses
with a vein-blue simplicity: here, shadows weave
through leaf and bristle: continuity in each breath:
the arc of a thrush punctuates the stillness, a syntax
of wings slicing air: the precision of flight:
each moment unfolding like a scroll onto the next,
the horizon a theorem proven by the setting sun:
and all equations find their place in the dirt path imprint,

gravity binding the fallen apple to its principles,
roots drinking deeply from the scripted well
of rain and decay: the cycle inscribed in a leaf:
so too do my thoughts find their orbit around
the permanence of change, stars in the vast churn:
my recognition a transient point on the endless curve
of being and becoming: each ending, a seed,
deposited in the fertile quiet of understanding:

thus blooms the inevitable, its beauty undeniable.
Leaves flutter down: cascades of decaying light,
patterns of loss and regrowth: natural
order in the foreclosed silence of an autumn
afternoon: the slow pull of earth, the spin
of decomposing: layers build, history
held tight in the humus and the heartbeat.

Forsaken Hymn no. 242

In this quiet, gaps widen:
her eyes, small pools where light dims,
reflect more than she says:
   leaves flutter outside the closed window,
     the world spins on without us,
and I, mute witness to her unraveling.

    Silence has weight, texture—
it fills our lungs like fine dust,
settles between us with the gravity
of celestial bodies unseen but felt,
orbits drawn in the air we breathe,
   the stuff of stars, the fabric of sorrows.

    Yet, in this shared solitude,
  a communion unfolds:
through the veil of tears, a bridge forms,
her pain mirrors mine,
   two spirits echoing in the void,
each echo a step closer to healing.

Forsaken Hymn no. 243

The sun cracks its whip across the horizon:
a spectrum ignites, fractals of light
    bouncing off the back of the morning tide,
    revealing every minute the imprint of time
as if the world speaks in shadows, sings
in the wavelengths between.

There is a science to this survival:
the persistence of waves carving rock,
the adaptable dance of shorebound weeds,
seabirds wheeling in the logic of updrafts;
all life attached by threads of carbon,
bound by the breath of an ancient star.

And so, I thread through the needle's eye
    of my own existence, stitching
the tapestry of what was with what will be,
    finding rhythm in the break of continuous waves,
   the certainty of a cycle that feels like hope—
    enough to coax the night into yielding, dawn reclaimed.

Forsaken Hymn no. 244

Here, the wind murmurs history:
old tales that span the gap between
gravity and the flight of dust:
  motions unseen, but deeply felt.
  From peak to valley, stories flow,
  each sediment a syllable.

The setting sun is not unlike
  a cooling core: its energy,
    once fierce and burning, now a soft,
luminous, lingering ache,
touching the hills with tenderness,
a gold seeker's final remorse.

Amid these stoic silences,
I sense a convergence of all
paths: what used to be and what will
    become blend in the quiet dusk.
Calamity's echo fades,
as earth turns from dusk into dark.

Forsaken Hymn no. 245

under the vast arch of sky: we see: all turns,
interlocks, like gears in the ceaseless clock
of the universe: where science sketches
   the boundaries of the known and the wilds
beyond it call to us with their silent,
singing mysteries.

   yet, we stand, finite, grasping at infinite
complexities: how a leaf, in falling,
traces algorithms of air and descent,
   or how water, in its eternal cycle,
shapes rock, carves valleys, feeds the thirsty
soil that bears our sustenance.

   so nature scripts its lessons in the scroll
of every unfurling fern, fiber of being:
teaching steadfastness amid flux,
   the kinship of chaos and cosmos,
that each ending begets a beginning:
and we, aware, must walk lightly here.

Forsaken Hymn no. 246

Leaves crunch underfoot: crisp pages
of autumn's final chapter, closing
with the cold's embrace: nature's bind,
tight as the chest when breath
turns visible in the dawn half-light,
every exhale a ghost joining the mist.

    And there: the horizon's blush hints
at a sun shy to climb, to claim
its place above the weary stretch
of land: does it too feel the tug,
reluctant to wake, to stir
    the sparrows from their silent perch?

    Winds whisper through skeletal trees,
branches like the fingers of a new father,
    reaching, unsure, trembling
      with the weight of their nakedness—
each twig a question in the cold,
and in the quiet, an answer forms.

Forsaken Hymn no. 247

The ship's hull groans: the sea's vast script
written in swells and troughs, the cold ink of depth:
each wave a line, relentless, not pausing
for a breath or thought, only pressing forward:
   this movement, a memory in water, forming,
      reforming, never the same twice over:

In the quiet below deck, Archie contemplates
the fractal chaos of his inner tides: how
   patterns emerge, complex and unpredictable,
like the mind's own spirals, echoing
the larger swells: this mirroring
of macrocosm in his pulse's rhythm:

   To engage with the ocean is to dialogue
     with the infinite, each response a wave's crest:
yet Archie finds the silent symmetry
     between the rolling deep and his restless heart,
    recognizing finally: all is flux, all is flow,
and in this flux, he, too, finds his echo.

Forsaken Hymn no. 248

In the hush of pre-dawn: silence speaks,
    its language, layered deep in the crisp chill
of air, where breath turns visible: a script
written by winter winds: that know
the contours of solitude: as clear
as a lone elm's shadow on untrodden snow.

Yet, amidst this quiet: a reminder swirls,
the chaos of day close at hand: the howl
    of morning's traffic like a river swollen
    with relentless rain: here, the stillness
yields, bending under the weight
of worlds waking: unasked, insistent.

But in this twilight, let me pause: treasure
    these moments that flicker: brief as the spark
from a flint: life, not in its clamor,
    but in the whisper of leaves: the slow
unfold of dawn across the sky: here,
    all ends meet: and stillness breathes anew.

Forsaken Hymn no. 249

In the cold note of rain: how each drop sings
   along the spine of time, like quicksilver
  forming rivulets: and how distinctly
this pavement, wet, reflects like a mirror
the trees bent in homage to brisk winds' calls,
susurrations of leaves composing hymns.

Between the arcs of car lights, shadows fall,
   rendering the ordinary sacred:
headlamps sketching truth on the night's vast wall,
      dispersed by mist, a scene perpetually
evolving as ideas in restless minds,
each glow a soft beacon in dimming times.

Here, under the hum of the universe,
wheels spin, pausing not for the lore of stars
nor the whispers of earthbound mysteries;
   driving away, the rearview grasps fragments
of what was, could be: in this fleeing view,
every end sews the seeds of a new start.

Forsaken Hymn no. 250

Winds shift: sands susurrate, distinct
  from the tumultuous sea: its surge
teaches us how to ebb, retreat,
to mimic quiet after squall.
The moon pulls: symphony of tides,
    orchestrating space between fullness
and void: a science of hollows—

akin to your laughter in empty rooms.
Atoms bond and break: our minutes
  are particles, scattered on the wind,
    echoes in the valley: shaping
the shapeless into a form.
Cycles spin: petals open at dawn,
    the sun each day new from the east,

transits the arc preordained:
each ending a slated rebirth.
So, I am but a shadow, moving
through phases, from new to full:
from emptiness to wonder, under
the arch of unending skies.

Forsaken Hymn no. 251

In every step: a narrative woven,
not just through soil and stone, but
through the veils of thoughts unspoken:
how each pulse in the crowded streets
echoes like a wave across the vast sea
of starlit skies and twilight whispers.

The leaves rustle a soft dialogue:
they speak of winds that have traveled
farther than our feet could ever wander,
breezing through tales of loss and find,
    their chlorophyll-rich veins mapping routes
we dream of, but pause too long to embark.

We are stitched into this endless fabric,
our shadows cast by city glow, rural dim,
colliding with the photons of forgotten suns:
each missed chance, a spark unseen,
draws a contour in the mind—deep, indelible—
and so completes the journey of our days.

Forsaken Hymn no. 252

    Lines on the globe: tracks left:
      by restless soles—I wonder
about the places that hold onto us
with invisible strings: gravity by other laws,
connections spelled in the circuitry
      of unseen roots and whispers.

    Within cells, atoms spin: the world
not still, even in the photograph—
time's illusion captured in still frame,
while everything moves as rivers do,
      shaping the banks they cannot see,
all life a series of returning tides.

And so, I circle back: remembering
    the breeze in Bhubaneswar,
how it carried the scent of rain and earth,
      a simple truth that we exist in layers, gathering,
each a stratum upon stratum: woven, complete—
    in the end, just travelers through each other's air.

Forsaken Hymn no. 253

Atoms mingle in the market's breath:
  each exhale a mesh of molecules,
new bonds form as old ones decay—
the subtle science of daily exchanges.
Here, amidst the clutter of commerce,
every coin flip is a quantum event:
  probabilities weighting the air,

  decisions dangling like ripe fruit.
Particles of us left behind,
on the worn cobblestones, fingerprints
invisible yet indelible: the commerce
of presence tying us to each place.
  In the dance of detachment and desire,

  each step marks a tracer of choices,
footprints that fade yet feed the grass
  growing stubborn through cracked pavements.
The vendor's eyes, weary windows
to souls bartered in silent symphonies,
  reflect the evening's orange glow:

Forsaken Hymn no. 254

In the lecture hall, light filters through
dust motes: our very own firmament:
    each particle a silent testimony
     to the ceaseless decay and renewal
that corners us, paradoxical:
sinew and thought intertwined.

Sister Maria nods, her eyes reflecting
the slide's glow: shadows of old texts
flickering on her face like soft flames:
here, the tangible meats the abstract,
melding thought with the visceral:
a quiet cataclysm of understanding.

The lessons dissolve into air, seasoned
with the tang of lemon, the slick of oil:
    as ideas steep, seep through the cracks
of consciousness, steeped in histories
we share, reshape, in breaths taken and given:
all ending in a whisper, not a clamor.

Forsaken Hymn no. 255

The leaf's edge curls: revelation,
  not decay, that all life turns in time
to show its veins stark against the sky's low blush,
each fracture: a map to the marrow of existence.
The creek stutters over cold stones
like thoughts tripping over themselves:
    how molecules clash and flow,

binding, parting: intimate strangers
  in the endless waltz of creation,
existence strung between starlight and silt.
In pulsing ecosystems, each breath merges
with another's, my twin soul's echo
  across the tangled underbrush—a thread
  that ties the silent music

    of our shared genesis to every crest
    and fall of the land we navigate together.
This dance of ours, dual yet singular,
embraces change as the constant consort,
where we share the blood of sunsets
    and the bones of deep-seated roots:

Forsaken Hymn no. 256

In silent corners, shadows dance;
the strands of Schubert float: each note
a cornerstone in the maze
of quiet thought, of lurking peace—
this Sunday room, sanctuary holding
both light and gloom: inviting contrasts.

Music swells, a tide against
the shore of chores undone, the pulse
of weeks worn thin: such spectral weights
hang heavy as the rain's relentless tap
against the pane, blending droplets
into streams, merging tasks with rhythmic dreams.

Yet here, in rest's paradoxical embrace,
swirling spirits mix with symphony,
contemplating peace as it ebbs and flows—
a divine puzzle, indifferent and immense,
overwhelming yet understated:
ending not in silence, but in song.

Forsaken Hymn no. 257

The storm speaks in a deep vibration:
its rumbles margining thoughts,
  shadows of oaks cast long stories
on the earth: here lies the quiet weight
    of old quarrels, undecided, hovering.
The air, thick with wet whispers, calls.

Leaves tremble, syllables in wind's grasp,
  each rustle a soft recollection
of a world that spins, unresolved:
conflict dripped through the hands of time,
    splattering patterns we try to read in the mud—
the roots, tangled, in silent discourse.

Storm clouds part, the horizon a clear line
drawn against the endless debates of sky:
each leaf now a witness to the cease
of rain, the clearing of human clatter.
  And I, caught between drops,
find respite in nature's quiet closure.

Forsaken Hymn no. 258

In this room where light shadows converge,
the clock's faint tick forms a rhythmic base
for Scarlatti's keys, notes lightly tossed
into the air: each a fleeting spark in the dim
    echoing softly against walls lined with the
spines of books, those quiet keepers of storm.

Each page a vessel, holding tight to the cries
of those who painted rhythms with their heart's
blood: Schubert, his melodies a weave of divine
agony, threads through the loom of despair,
    his pain stitched within bars of transcendent
sound, persisting as unchanged as stone figures.

Yet here, amid these muffled scholarly whispers,
where thoughts tangle with the music of ages,
I grasp the frail thread of creation's pulse:
how art extends beyond the brittle edges
of our lives, binding us in a silent continuity,
    where even now, the notes resonate, complete.

Forsaken Hymn no. 259

In the shaded aisle: the onset of twilight,
   murmur of pages turning: soft as leaf fall.
  Here, your arguments linger: notes in the margin,
dense as forest, sharp as cut stone.
  Your words, articulated with a clarity:
crisp like the snap of winter branches—
a continuity unbroken: even as shadows stretch,

even as the ink fades on paper thin as moth wings.
  Amid the rows, I seek your logic,
wrestle with the echo of your thesis,
a dialogue renewed beneath the whispering fans.
Aren't these debates—ghostly, yet fervent—
markers of our undying quests?
Here in the half-light, I sense your retort

threading through the stale air: charged,
ready to ignite new thoughts on old fires.
Yes, in this confluence of past and present,
  I find not an end, but an invitation:
  a call to delve deeper into the flux
of a world you left richer than you found.

Forsaken Hymn no. 260

At sixty, the spine of the mountain
teaches me the rigor of stone:
each layer, sedimented with time's insistence,
compresses—folds—holds tight the fossil musings
of ancient sunlight and decayed forms—
my days, too, layer under the weight of hours.
Life's lattice, like mineral veins through hard quartz,
draws silver threads: pathways, labyrinthine

and furtive, where thought delves deep, seeking
   the bright ore of understanding.
In the weave of the wind, I hear
the leaf's rustle: a dialect for the air's caress,
   the tree's patient turning toward the light.
Branches compose a fractal score,
symphony of ongoingness, the pulse—

steady, yet swayed by breezes' whims.
Through this arboreal dance, insights
swell like buds into leaves, into history.
   In the silence of growth, I grasp
the infinite, rooted yet reaching—
beneath soil, above sky—my existence
boundless as the cycle of seasons.

Forsaken Hymn no. 261

In this breath we hold, between ascent
and the soft, inevitable decline: the arc
of a life shadowed by clouds, cumulus
heavy with the whisper of rain: how it speaks
   of change, transient yet persistent, demanding
the attention of the grounded and the aloft.

   Each drop forms and falls: a minute history
of atmosphere's embrace: gravity's quiet claim
   on the vapor-born back to the earth: a cycle
   a science, yet felt deeply as any beat
of heart, or the pulse of ink flowing
from pen to paper, scripting the unseen.

So, here, with a pen's tip that dances, curves
on the ample belly of the page, landing softly—
   each word a touch, a breath upon the white;
enough to stir the trees outside, to swirl
the leaves in their perpetual waltzing flight—
until at rest, all is written, and all returns right.

Forsaken Hymn no. 262

In the quiet calculus of our separation,
each equation unbalanced: you, subtracted,
leaving a remainder heavy as winter clouds.
Your echo pulses through the leafless trees,
a theorem of absence: undefined, yet clear,
the thin air crisp with the algebra of cold—
here, where frost sketches arcane glyphs

on window glass, nature's own cipher writing
messages in the moisture of our mingled breaths,
once warm and close, now dissipated like mist.
I trace the geometry of lost pathways,
where our words had danced in delicate symmetry,
   and silence now grows, exponential, a curve
    steeping sharply towards infinity.

In this quiet, all things converge:
   your absence a constant, unyielding, complete.
    The cosmos watches, vast and unblinking,
    its cold eye indifferent to our shrinking,
as we, small and solitary,
navigate the vastness of the void:

Forsaken Hymn no. 263

In dimming woods, paths wind unseen:
the crunch of dry leaves mark my pace.
Heartbeats align with quieter scenes,
wisdom etched deep within my face.
Each step, a mixture of echo and intent,
maps not the land, but the heart's contour.

The territory of the soul extends,
threads through each withered leaf, each stone.
As twilight deepens, shadows blend,
  our lives, their meanings, softly thrown
into relief: each crumple, each bend,
a narrative of flesh and bone.

Time's embrace, gentle yet unyielding,
guides my stride towards realms anew.
Through layers of leaf and years, wielding
lessons gathered in morning dew,
the end of paths, where maps cease:
here lies peace, in the knowing of release.

Forsaken Hymn no. 264

As time marches, so do thoughts: unfurled,
tangling in the limbs of oak and elm,
   each leaf a syllable, weathered and worn:
like pages in the wind, scattered stories settling.
Sunset translates the day into hues
   of quiet introspection: how the light
     bends at the horizon, gathering
  the age in cool, blue shadows,

tracing the slow descent
   of fire into ember.
Memory—those sharp, bright shards—
breaks against the shore of now,
where I collect these smoothed stones,
evidence of a younger self's fierce tides:
   the fervor and the folly, captured

in the calm pools of quieter waters.
Here, the past whispers through the reeds,
the voices of Connolly, of Pearse,
   not lost but layered,
deep beneath the still surface,
their convictions sedimented
   into the bedrock of my being.

Forsaken Hymn no. 265

In twilight's hush, a leaf whispers to stone:
its journey, simple, tumbling from the branch:
  not just a fall, but through the air, a dance
maneuvered by the wind's unseen hand, alone
in ways that mimic my strides: unpredictable,
each step a claim on unmarked paths, a script:

The world spins—not just on its axis—:
but also on the edges of our comprehension,
  each revelation a turnover of soil, rich
with decay and sprouting new inquiries:
where does the boundary lie between
chaos and cosmos if not in our grasp?

Under moon's cool glance, my thoughts
pivot like planets orbiting a sun unseen;
the natural order—a clock wound by unseen
forces—ticks in the silence of growing shadows:
finding peace not in certainty but in acceptance,
each ending a node in the web of perpetual beginnings.

Forsaken Hymn no. 266

In twilight's thinning breath, the veil lifts:
each step presses a memory into the earth,
    where footfalls echo Archie's faded path—
his name, a silent flutter against the cosmos,
drifting farther from the touch of hands
that once clung to his presence like roots.

Leaves whisper the weight of absence,
    their rustle a manuscript of the unseen,
scripting the air with particles of the past:
how light bends around the forgotten,
    and shadows cast by nothing leave
an imprint deeper than existence.

    Yet, in this interstitial silence, a belief:
that every loss sews seeds of being,
    the universe knitting voids into constellations,
stars named and unnamed, weaving
the dark with threads of forgotten light—
each glow a quiet defiance of the end.

Forsaken Hymn no. 267

The wind shifts: a murmur through the leaves:
  Louis seems near, spectral in the twilight:
his essence not lost but absorbed,
deep into the fabric of this park,
where light plays on the old sycamores:
each leaf a silent witness to our days.

  Our conversations drift on a breeze:
    he'd argue, life is a series of climbs,
      each more daunting yet, strangely, needed:
    his camera capturing more than sights,
      it seized the essence of fleeting moments,
turning the ephemeral to eternal.

So, as I watch dusk embrace the earth,
and shadows merge into a gentle dark,
I find comfort in knowing: Louis climbs still,
    not up mountains, but within minds,
his legacy a beacon: a reminder
that we, too, can reach beyond our grasp.

Forsaken Hymn no. 268

Before dawn, the cosmos whispers:
its nebulous chill breathes stories
of Archie, his laughter once vibrant,
now a softer glow against the quiet
landscape of remembrance and loss:
both binding us in invisible threads.

  Through the window, Orion shifts,
   his belt aligning with faint horizons:
a reminder of cycles, the eternal
spinning of earth and stars:
how we reach, through the veil of night,
     toward the uncertain embrace of dawn.

    Soon, sunlight scripts the hills,
each beam a verse in the syntax
of renewal: how light returns,
forgiveness: a landscape reformed.
Eternal, the day asserts its bright claim,
our spirits reconciled with the turning earth.

Forsaken Hymn no. 269

In twilight's soft decline, elements blend:
   carbon with dusk, the chatter of photons
escaping the pull of a dense nucleus
where forces both create and consume.
   The wind whispers through the ferns,
particles in flux, the lore of motion:
each leaf's twist a theorem, proven

by the tilt and weave of passing breezes.
Atoms, those minuscule dancers, spin
   in the vast ballet of space, pairing
   and parting: a cosmic choreography
guided by the unseen hand of laws.
   Sequences unfold in the script of stars,
recitations of light across the void,

   their stories written in the wavelength
of their journey through night's canvas.
In the pause of earthly hours,
where thoughts collide with the silence
of growing shadows, I read the patterns
left by time's subtle feet.

Forsaken Hymn no. 270

In this garden, life whispers: grow, decay:
hushed beneath each tread, soft as ancient lore,
bewitched earth, twirling time with her array:
    each petal falls, yet hinting at the core
    of boundless cycle, tugging at the hem
of my thoughts, seasoned by the drum's deep beat.
A leaf drifts, cradling the sun's last gem,

caught in the subtle play of light and heat.
Is this not the pulse of existence: bold,
continuous, a threading of quiet?
All, under the drum's ceaseless rhythm, hold
firm to the dance of day slipping to night,
every ending sewn with a fresh start,
    lacing through the fabric of heart to heart.

    So, the solitary drummer pounds on,
his echoes a scaffold through time and space,
an eternal calling, dusk to dawn,
where we see life's lines, softly interlace.
    Wandering paths converge in understood
silence, completing the cycle: all is good.

Forsaken Hymn no. 271

In the tides of cloud shapes: each form
   signals a shift: the lamb leaps,
   the dove dives: stories woven in vapor,
tales that dance on the whim of the wind:
how fleeting, yet how deeply they carve
our inner recesses with old, wordless knowledge.

See, in the birthing sky, a narrative unfolds:
   soft morphs, the artistry of atmosphere,
   brushing the canvas of the blue infinite:
each change a mimic of life's own mutations,
reflective of the subtle births and quiet deaths
   that mark the time of a day, a life, a world.

   And I, grounded, yet grasping at the ethereal—
each cloud a symbol, each drift a destiny—
in the broad sweep of sky, a connection:
a breath shared with the infinite,
a mirror to my own transient breath;
in this, the closure of a loop, the peace of partaking.

Forsaken Hymn no. 272

Beneath the moon's quiet curve,
thoughts unfurl: tendrils of vine
   grip to worn stone, where time
etches deep histories. The air:
cold, telling of dusk's secrets,
whispers of decay and renewal.
   By the edge, I balance: not fully
possessing, nor fully possessed,

a midpoint in gravity's gentle
clasp: the moon tugs
   at ocean's expansive breast,
as stars chart the dim path forward.
   Claws prick gently at my shoulder:
reminders that all weight is shared,
   even as Archie fades into mist—
his last words scattering, trying

to tell us something about loss,
   momentum, and the fine dust of stars.
Each line we draw in the cosmos,
faint yet determined, seeks connection
  in the vast dark: we are but echoes
  in the void, dancing particles in light
    and shadow, bound by the unseen
   threads we weave together.

Forsaken Hymn no. 273

The land stretches: austere, expansive,
cracked—here, where the oil-drenched
earth bleeds black beneath the tread
of luxury: the silent testimony
of engines, their roar muted
   by the vast, swallowing desert.

   Yet, in this severe opulence, a thought:
the sun, relentless, mirrors our own
unyielding drives: necessity, survival:
   etched not only in the sand
   but also in the sinews of those
   who pace the perimeters of power.

What binds us, here, under the sear
   of distant suns? Much more than
   chains or the whispers of transaction.
We thread through the canopy of stars,
wrestling with shadows cast
by our own making, until the end: complete.

Forsaken Hymn no. 274

In the cool pause of night's mantle,
the universe shrinks to a murmur:
  quiet thoughts weave through the cosmos,
stars flicker, drafting light in ancient codes.
The crickets' hymn twists through the grass,
nodes of life vibrating with raw frequency;
each blade of green tuned to the earth's pulse,

the soil's breath—deep, rhythmic, slow:
Continents drift, their burdens worn like crowns,
ice melts, waters rise: everything is flux
and reflux—the ceaseless motion of being,
one wave folding into the next in endless dialogue.
Now, I stand where the sky meets the prairie,
  contemplating the blend of dark soil with my fingers.

  The land stretches, patient and unyielding,
its truths buried deep in marl and loam:
Roots twist downward, anchoring dreams,
  leaves reach outward—brush strokes of survival.
Here, I find the firm ground of belonging,
my spirit anchored in the weave of nature's fabric.

Forsaken Hymn no. 275

In the warmth of lecture halls I unfold,
discourse swirling like an unseen galaxy:
every chair-foot's scrape, a minor quake
   that stirs not dust but starlit curiosity.
The echo of wood on floorboards, a pulse
  pounding through the veneer of order:
here, science meets the spirit's dance in discourse,

    each movement a test, a trial of borders.
Yet, as Orion shifts weight from one leg to another,
our minds drift beyond the celestial wheel:
we are not only learners but cosmos's children,
  scratching at the edges of the great unknown.
Whiskey in hand, I propose a toast to chaos:

    to the beauty found in stirring the air,
   to the freedom in the fall of a boundary,
where every collision crafts new worlds.
  And so we converge in shared oscillation,
weaving through the fabric of theories and thoughts:

Forsaken Hymn no. 276

"I am home.": The tether snaps back,
pulled by the gravity of old haunts,
yet I am adrift, a leaf on Dublin's rush-hour river,
flowing past the pungent taverns and age-worn stones
where new faces blur into the roles of old friends,
and laughter spills like ale into the night.

   The city pulses around me: each beat
a fragment of a long-lost echo
that I strain to hear over the din
of my own solitude: Dublin's cobbled veins
channel the ceaseless stream of partings and returns,
a lattice of absence braided with presence.

Here, in the quiet aftermath, a truth surfaces,
quiet and clear as the lilt of a lonesome fiddle—
freedom lies not in the flight
but in the finding: each step
an arrival, each breath a homecoming:
thus ends my quest, here, heart saying at last, "I am home."

Forsaken Hymn no. 277

In the shadow of the great oak's whisper,
    the science of decay is not lost on me:
molecules break and recombine, a constant
flux, a dance of detachment and reunion:
    as roots delve deep, seeking, always seeking,
the moist nurture of a dark earth.

Around us, the architecture of lives
    constructed in the brief light of day—
a blueprint, fragile yet fervent:
    walls echo with the laughter of years,
    and floors wear the patina of countless
footsteps, each a tiny impact in time.

And here, between the sigh of the old,
and the eager pulse of the new:
my heart archives every whisper,
each a filament within the web of memory,
    linking me to you: and as I step forward,
the chorus of life persists, unbroken.

Forsaken Hymn no. 278

In the dimming light, leaves whisper:
each a chapter in the saga of survival,
where the softest murk fosters fierce blooms:
nature's meticulous, relentless crafting.
These gentle giants, rooted yet reaching,
breathe in the twilight's chalky coolness:
their limbs stretch, caress the coming night,

a ballet of shadows on the earthen stage.
 Every rustle a verse in the lore of persistence,
the art of enduring woven through the veins
of each sagging, tired petal fighting dusk.
And here I stand, caught in the web
of this ceaseless transformation:
from soil to leaf, from seed to shade.

I am not apart from this, but a piece:
 rooted in the cycles that wheel ceaselessly.
As Archie's words blend into the winds,
a reminder that all departures fold into arrivals,
with the queen bee's flight etched deep
 in the patterns of our own, perpetual migrations.

Forsaken Hymn no. 279

In the chill of dawn: each wave a new
chapter, the horizon unfolds stories
   as if pages, stirred by the breath of gods;
and my companions, bound in leather and promise,
slumbering giants of thought and dream,
await the warmth of my seeking hands.

   The sea speaks in tongues of salt and brine,
      each froth-tipped message: a fragment of the vast,
spun from the loom of the deep, where light
dwindles, and mysteries dwell in cold suspension;
here, crashing against the finite sands,
they translate into the idiom of the now.

   I hold close the wisdom of Whitman, Dante—
      vast echoes in the chambers of my soul.
Guided by celestial hands unseen,
my course charts through waters deep and wild,
   each line I write: a vow, a breath, a step
toward the shores where all stories rest.

Forsaken Hymn no. 280

At the brink of vast seas, I ponder:
  the pull of tide, the moon's quiet command,
how water shapes the shore, and life:
    endlessly worn, yet persistently reborn.
Molecules merge and drift apart:
unity and division in a fluid dance.

Paths unfold across continents
like veins under the skin of the earth,
    pulsing with the lifeblood of passage.
    Here, one step forwards, the old ground fades,
the echo of resolve in each footprint,
new soil beneath my feet whispering welcome.

In this departure, connections emerge:
    every goodbye laced with the potential of hello,
the stretch of my spirit towards uncharted joys.
    Stitched into the vast quilt of existence,
  where every fabric tells a tale,
    I find closure in the open-ended journey.

Forsaken Hymn no. 281

In the cool drift of evening's claim,
each wave: a soft, relentless force
    that sculpts the shore's unending frame,
a cycle, set, without remorse.
Yet, each curve holds a novel form,
echoes in the sand, fine and warm.
Across the space, between the stars,
the sky expands: a deep exhale,

    while gulls, in their unscripted wars,
weave narratives on gusty trails.
The night's embrace tightens, profound,
as dusk's colors begin to drown.
Beneath these vast celestial streams,
I find myself within their fold,
transfixed by infinite extremes:

of stories told, retold, untold.
    In this dance of eternal lights,
I grasp at fleeting, final sights.
As silence sets and thoughts take flight,
cradled by the whispering tide,
    I see how endings are but slight
pauses in rhythms, far and wide.

Forsaken Hymn no. 282

In the vast expanse, alone but not:
  each wave a memory inked and caught
as it breaks upon the stern, reflecting
much of Archie's thinking—
how ideas, like currents, reshape sands
of minds across disparate lands:
their words, looping back like the tide,

feed newer thoughts that will not bide
  within the strict confines of the old.
The sea whispers, lessons retold
in foamy laces, intricate and brief,
  on the hull of this solitary reef.
Beneath the sky's immensity,
I find a semblance of constancy,

despite the endless shift and play
  of ocean's deep, where mysteries stay.
  What remains as my companions fade?
  The threadbare rope, its strength decayed,
still hints at a weave, once tight and bold—
  like tales of the spirit, not growing old,
  but rewoven in the mesh of now:

Forsaken Hymn no. 283

In the dark, stars hidden, yet present:
unseen guides charting paths through
an endless, celestial drift—
echoes of a distant bar's hum,
a terrestrial undertone to the cosmic silence,
reminding us: all moments merge here.

The continuum of a ship slicing night seas,
   passengers held tight in their hopeful fears,
replaying scenes of potential,
each life a narrative spun from joy and despair—
infinite stories navigating the currents,
   each story a wave, rising, then swallowed.

Archie, at twenty-one, understood—
the future a tapestry woven from past threads;
each memory a stitch in the grand design.
And now, those youthful days, submerged in time,
come washing back in a flood of insight:
Life's worth, measured in the weight of its echoes.

Forsaken Hymn no. 284

Earth spins, a dark thread winding the sun:
each morn, it stitches gold across the horizon,
 the fray of night pulled tight by radiant hands.
Nature conducts its ceaseless tableau:
a leaf's vein pulsing with chlorophyll-laced blood,
  a seagull's cry slicing the salty air.

 Archie's sparse grins fracture the silence—
the brief spark of connection in a woven mesh
of faces fleeting, voices a fleeting murmur.
Isolation, too, has its own physics:
atoms apart yet bound by invisible forces,
seeking bonds in the void's endless gap.

Yet, continuity prevails, even in departure,
 as we drift from youthful shores
to test the depths of more ancient waters.
 The final stitch is a gentle closure:
not the end, but a merging into the vast,
eternal tapestry where every thread has a place.

Forsaken Hymn no. 285

   Morning stretches its long fingers
    through the canopy: light diffuses,
soft as it touches the dew-laden leaves,
and I think: this is the process of awakening,
both of the forest and of my own encased spirit,
dense as the dark soil, potent with gestation.

The silence isn't empty: it hums, vibrating
with the latent promise of life,
   like the resonance in the chambers
of a seashell: each spiral, a story
of depths plumbed and surfaces skimmed;
    and in my ear, the ocean's distant calling.

Paths wind into the unseen,
and I—with each step—entangle further
with the web of existence: complex,
unyielding, yet as fragile as the spider's silk,
that glistens in the new sun.
Here ends my journey, not with closure, but with connection.

Forsaken Hymn no. 286

In the pulse of faded corridors,
echoes trace the steps of loss:
each footfall—a subdued drum,
the rhythm bleak, the beat goes on,
hushed, yet certain as the flow
of time through the narrowing isthmus.

Life, a series of closing doors,
each threshold crossed with less ceremony,
every room—a silent witness to the wait,
or the swift departure of breath,
while nurses move like shades,
tending the quietus with soft hands.

What truths do we glean from this gloom—
   charting paths where light seldom intrudes?
The dance of life and decay,
    under the stark fluorescence, I pause—
searching for a small spark in the murk,
finding peace in the final line of the story.

Forsaken Hymn no. 287

In the quiet shift, a snake slips
from old skin: a glistening fresh
form revealed in shadowy damp:
   thrives free from the heavy coat
of past seasons: under a sun
that whispers its light through leaves:
   each beam a gentle guide, not a glare:

meticulous touch of warming
   rays: the snake basks, half-hidden,
half-open to the world's soft gaze:
in this dance of light and shadow,
change breathes a subtle rhythm:
each beat a quiet step, a soft unfolding,
   life whispers through the underbrush:

a delicate balance: quietness completes.
   In the quiet movement of Archie's molt,
skin sloughs off: silent testimony to change,
   a snake leaving behind what it cannot carry:
shed scales like shed fears, unnoticed yet
integral to growth, to survival.

Forsaken Hymn no. 288

Amid clamor and din: I walk, ears besieged,
A heart in the whirl: survival or peace?
Each step, a yes: balancing fragile truce,
Between life's chaos: and its stark ceases.
Threads of good tangled: with threads of less good,
A fabric woven: on the loom of days,
    A question of being, stark in its asking:

To serve or to stand, in these fraying ways.
Through streets etched with struggle, our histories mark,
Hungarian smiles bearing burdens from past,
Each grin, a story: resilience whispered,
In the face of long shadows, overcast.
Grappling with existence: slopes icy, steep,
Voices chant, 'Serve, Serve,' into the deep night,

Fists clenched, not in anger but holding tight:
To the promise of dawn, however slight.
And so I navigate, urban tightrope taut,
Where the dance of 'yes' murmurs beneath feet,
Navigating life's jagged edge: find peace,
    In the heart's quiet song, amidst the beat.

Forsaken Hymn no. 289

In the soft edges of day, she stands:
a figure melded from sea breeze and light,
    her laughter, a chord strung through the crashing
       waves: a resonance, lifting the gulls beyond.
    Her eyes, a science of their own, reflect
the boundless gray of turning tides where time
    collapses into the rhythm of water,

threading silver through the loom of the horizon.
  With each step, the sand adopts her imprint:
a temporary claim, soon to be swept
away by evening's diligent hands, yet
her essence—a revolution, persists.
In the murmur of waves, I discern
    the pulse of nature's vast manuscript,

      writing itself over: eras, epochs—
    her presence a footnote, yet pivotal.
As dusk cloaks the air with its velvet sigh,
we are mere shadows against the vast ink
of ocean, drawn together, drawn apart,
in the dance of existence and retreat.

Forsaken Hymn no. 290

The rain speaks: patter, patter, drop:
    each syllable a cool whisper on leaves,
  an ancient dialect, Ireland's own,
where history seeps into the soaked earth,
mingling past with the present: continuous,
a fluid manuscript written in green ink.

Here, moisture clings to each blade of grass,
    like memory sticks to the bones of the old,
each droplet reflects a story: Joyce's streams,
Yeats' winding stair, Synge's quiet islands,
drenched in a mist that veils and reveals,
nature's breath a damp sigh on my cheeks.

And Iowa, with its fields, vast and open,
tells a different tale under the same sky,
where soil turns under the plow, life cycles
through growth and decay: corn and swine,
    all seeking, like us, their place under the sun,
a quiet recognition in the heart's sprawling fields.

Forsaken Hymn no. 291

The golden fur, tangled in brambles:
how her stillness met the earth, resonant
   as if listening, though the heart had ceased.
Bear shadows lumbered, outlines of instinct,
carved from the dense fabric of the forest,
their movements—raw scripts of need and survival.

Branches crack under the weight of simple truths:
life grinds on, blind to the significance
   of one fallen heroine in the wild.
   Here, death and life entwine like twisted roots:
the promise of decay feeds the blooming,
and what falls away nourishes the soil.

In the chill air, my breath sketches ghosts,
each exhale a reminder of the fragile ties
that bind us to these beasts, these trees, this ground.
And in this woven tapestry of breath and bone,
   we find the harsh grace of being: alive, aware,
   in a world that moves with or without us.

Forsaken Hymn no. 292

In the low hum of the pub, time ebbs:
solitude is a shawl, draped loosely
  around the shoulders of night.
Each tick of the clock melds into
  the rhythm: rain on the tin roof,
patter syncopated by gusts.

The whiskey burns, a fiery trace
  that lingers as thoughts of Archie,
    who danced with fate, fingertips
  tracing the edge of each revel,
his laughter—a cloak that hid
his churning, shadowed depths.

  Here, the whisper of glass on wood,
soft as dreams that fleet onwards,
reminds us: all is interwoven,
    fate and chance stitch the hours
  into garments we barely perceive;
and in this dance, we find peace.

Forsaken Hymn no. 293

In the weave of light and shadow, I navigate:
 each thought a filament caught in the vast
net of the cosmos, pulling at the seams
  of the unknown: how each thread intertwines,
a tapestry of chaos and cosmos meticulously
forged by the pulse of existence.

 The echo of the infant's cry, a frequency
  that ripples through the fabric of being,
reminding us: the origins of our insights
  are not silent, nor are they ever still:
movement—the constant hum of energy
  that propels us, relentless and urgent.

 We, seekers on paths less trodden,
  must balance finely on the beam of now,
where past is a whisper and future—a shout,
and every step a stitch in the span of time.
 In the end, the dance slows, each turn
  a complete thought: serene, sublime.

Forsaken Hymn no. 294

In the scattered aftermath:
each shard of glass casts back,
   not just light, not just my fractured stare,
but tiny spectrums of a truth I'm tracing,
   where colors bend at the edge of understanding,
and thought itself becomes luminous, elusive.

Amidst these prisms, a pattern:
the deliberate art of breaking,
   to rebuild from splinters,
like the forest regenerates after fire,
roots deeper for the disturbance,
life's insistence weaving through decay.

What then, of this wreckage?
   Each piece, once part of a greater whole,
   now mirrors a segment of sky—
      reflecting not what is, but what could be:
a mosaic of potential, painful, yet pure,
the landscape of a new vision, finally complete.

Forsaken Hymn no. 295

In the quiet unraveling of evening,
the horizon blurs: light dips,
heavy in the lap of the water,
a seamless melding, like thoughts
  adrift in the immensity of dusk:
each connection, a thread woven.

In my garden, the peat moss holds
whispers, the dark earth spongy,
yielding: beneath my fingers,
roots and seeds—my dreams
cast in the loam, praying for sprout,
  echoing the pulse of tender burials.

Above, the sky darkens, pulling
stars from the well of night:
each a pinprick in the fabric
of the cosmos, threading light
  across the void: here,
in the communion of shadow and soil.

Forsaken Hymn no. 296

Beneath the stretch of the afternoon sky,
where the horizon melts: blue into more blue,
I find the curvature of earth, hidden—
    like thoughts half-formed, disappearing
    into the vastness of quiet breathing:
    sea air, mixed with the scent of early rain.

The garden leaves whisper, Archie's soft tread
among damp petals: each step a small echo
of distant places—threaded by dreams,
    longing, the touch of the unseen:
how each leaf gathers dew, gravity's gentle
    call, pooling connections unseen.

In this network of roots and canopy,
where fear meets grace: the balance held
    tight like the grip of earth on seed—
    here, I rest in the complete thought,
the cycle closed, like a cat curling
where sunlight warms the old wood floor.

Forsaken Hymn no. 297

The river speaks of continuity:
its flow, the ceaseless dialogue of droplets,
each merge a story of persistence,
each parting a testament to change.
Here, where the Liffey mirrors castles,
both crumbled yet standing tall:

in reflection, broken yet whole,
Archie and I, not warriors but craftsmen,
fashioning from shards not spears but shields,
the golden mail of quiet days
woven tight with strands of self
amidst the ruins of what we were:

my mind, a riverbed, eroded yet enriched
by every thought that waters tread.
The pulse of creation—a thrum, a ache—
how it resists the calm, the safe!
In the murmur of the Liffey's course,
I am repaired, whole: the journey done.

Forsaken Hymn no. 298

The screen's flicker: a ghostly dance
of photons: Archie's presence captured,
his laugh a clip replayed, decaying
   into the soft buzz of my dark room:
outside, the hush of twilight seeping
through cracks, as if trying to witness.

This absorption of day into night
mirrors Archie, shifting: now flesh,
now mere image, replayed, paused,
silent amidst the hum of passing cars:
   his daughter's eyes, wide in the glow,
      capture the pulse of unseen stars.

   And in this quiet, I reconcile:
myself with the shadows cast on walls,
the impermanent mark of my words,
like his, filtered through endless noise:
yet in the stillness, we exist,
complete, as the night folds us home.

Forsaken Hymn no. 299

Changes loom: both dreaded and embraced,
like river banks eroded under relentless flow,
the earth: it shifts imperceptibly beneath,
and we—though small—observe this dance of dust:
   a cosmos in constant negotiation
with the forces that shape its skin.

Through microscopes, I see the intricate
detail: cells divide, each one a universe,
propelled by unseen energies that compel
their harmony or chaos: so too my thoughts,
scattered like autumn leaves across the landscape
of my restless ambitions.

   I walk through this city of contrasts,
of sharp corners and soft, decaying petals,
each step a stitching in the fabric
of my existential quilt: I am part
of this process: a fragment of the whole,
finding peace in the cycle's close.

Forsaken Hymn no. 300

The branches arc, skyward and splayed:
ghosts of the old oaks in my youth,
  their whispers rustle through the leaves,
  a murmuring of time's aloof
  indifference to fleeting breath.
    In each leaf's vein: a history.

Old stone faces, stern and silent,
etched by the chisel of the wind:
they preach in the language of stillness,
    towering over me, mere kin
to the moss that clings and claims—
    the slow, enduring grasp of change.

  I ponder, here, beneath this span
of green and granite, time's slow art:
the sculpting of a human heart,
constancy in a fleeting part,
how I am both the moving and
the still, at rest with where I stand.

Forsaken Hymn no. 301

In the frosty echo of leaf-crunch:
we tread, feet whispering through
the underbrush, where light slivers
    slice the dense canopy above:
each ray, a storyline,
each shadow, a silent retort.

  Here, where the soil holds
the chill of night longer than the sky—
    earth's persistence: to cradle seed and worm,
legacy in layers: humus, heartache, homecoming,
    roots threading through histories,
woven tight as destiny's fabric.

Amid these ancient stands, our brief passages
seem fleeting, thoughts like spores
released into the wind—
wisdom or folly: the forest absorbs both,
leaving us bare, faced with only our essence,
until the path clears, and we step into open light.

Forsaken Hymn no. 302

In O'Connell's lounge: conversations curl,
   like smoke: whispers and laughter blend,
the warmth of shared spaces: an echo of lives
   intertwined: Archie nods, his rhythm steady,
a counterpoint to fleeting giggles,
   the child's delight in simple moments.

   Outside, the Irish rain speaks a steady pulse:
tap against glass, a pattern of nature's own,
matching inner storms: here, reflections ripple,
   mirroring the complexities of hearts and days
entangled: love's deep weave, loss's sharp edge,
   threads drawn tight, the fabric of our shared existence.

Sandy watches, counts—three whispers in heaven—
each a soft footprint on the damp earth of memory,
while life spins on, its ceaseless cycles: grains
in the vast hourglass, sifted, layered,
until all that's left is the essence, distilled:
bare, yet full: the completeness of being.

Forsaken Hymn no. 303

Each step, a note in the symphony of twilight:
paths diverge and converge, like streams
    meeting and parting: isn't it just so, how thoughts
tangle as vines in the fertile soil of the mind,
each idea germinating from the decay of another,
roots touching in the dark, unseen but essential.

Consider Sandy: her visions sown deep, sprouting
in the currency of leaves, photosynthesizing
        complexities into the green simplicity of spring.
    And David, reflecting not the sun but the moon's
pale inquiry, serene in the still surface tension
of her own making: her nature, a quiet lake.

In the cooling air, my mother's voice carries from
her northern perch, safeguarding flames that flicker
against the encroaching night: friend or family,
a pinpoint of light in the vast dark, connected
by more than mere chance or casual glance,
    fostering warmth that grows as the day closes.

Forsaken Hymn no. 304

Here, in reflection's fire-lit embrace:
the shadows dance—a pageantry of dark
   and light, where thoughts like penguins arc,
each white crest breaking dawn's icy face.
   The flame, a flicker in the sturdy night,
conjures forms: Archie and Bigfoot too,
melding real with unreal, old views

and legends, the boundary lines blurred just right.
   Archie sang of gin's infinite shapes,
while I trace slow paths through quicker songs,
finding truth where the heart long belongs,
      in the weave of life, where no thread escapes.
This narrative, spun from fire's soft glow,

patterns the cloth of existence, soul-sewn.
   Each moment, a stitch; time's vast unknown
is ours to quilt, to mend, to know.
By firelight, with patience time has honed,
we sit, the night's fabric finely interwoven,
completing, at last, this circle, time-proven:

Forsaken Hymn no. 305

In the autumn sway, leaves whisper:
the cycle of fervor and fade,
each one a syllable in nature's long dialogue
   with the sun, with the soil: from the vigor
to the drooping, a dance of daylight and decay.
Beneath the moon's cool gaze, I walk—

cobblestones, slick with mossy rain, remember
   my stride, the same one that slipped
    and twisted in the grip of youthful audacity:
all of nature, a giant inhaling before the plunge
into the somber frost of winter.
And in the final embers of daylight,

as shadows stretch to claim their ancient territory,
   I contemplate the passage: from fire to ash,
    casting long thoughts back to those flames
that once cut through fog, marking beginnings
   and endings, a beacon's relentless message:
within every end, a spark of the new.

Forsaken Hymn no. 306

In this landscape, the horizon bends:
not just with the curvature of earth,
but with the weight of time itself—
how it molds the airy whispers
into voices thick with peat and rain,
how it sculpts the hills, green-veined
 and pulsing with histories alive:

echoes of monks, their laughter
spun into the wind's cool thread,
a tapestry of mossy stones and mire.
Here, I find the measure of home
not in the structures men build,
but in the slow, persistent song
 of earth bedding rock—quiet, vast,

the kind of quiet that speaks
and lends weight to my own voice,
 as if I, too, might echo through time,
rooted and ephemeral, like the dance
of sun-fire caught on the undersides
 of clouds at dusk: ending, always,
in the silent promise of renewal.

Forsaken Hymn no. 307

In the quiet of books and muffled sighs,
each spine a backbone: stories, lives,
lined up, their tales woven into each other:
how do we measure the weight of a whisper,
　　the depth at which a laughter sinks,
or the silence after a page turns,
sudden, like soft thuds of heartbeats
muffled under the skin of days,

each tick another stitch in the fabric
　of our collected selves, dappled
by the light filtering through old glass?
　　Here, amid the creaks and cracks,
a child's voice lifts, crystalline, breaking
　　through the murk of grown murmurs,
its innocence a blade slicing
through dense air, clear and bright,

　　as if to remind us: remember simplicity.
In the resonance of these young echoes,
　　we find clarity—like water cupped in hands,
　its coolness a small truth against our lips,
and the world, with all its spun complexities,
grasps at these fleeting, pristine moments—
how we linger, finally, at the threshold of understanding.

Forsaken Hymn no. 308

Amid the drifts of fallen leaves:
each crunch a whisper of the past,
the crisp decay shakes loose the weight
of history pressed deep in pages
and damp earth: the scent of endings
and beginnings mixed, interwoven.

    The leaves, thin veils over the hard
      pavement, flutter like the weak pulse
of time itself: here galls, there buds,
      sprouting from the cracked spine of a book
    overlooked, where heroes' dreams are penned—
      fallen, yet echoing still in leaf-rustle.

Their names—O'Rahilly to Pearse—resound
    in the shuffle of my steps, echo
in each leaf's turn from green to gold,
    and there, in the cool despair, I find
contemplation, the seamless thread
binding us with the stubbornness of hope.

Forsaken Hymn no. 309

In this quiet, where thoughts echo:
minds, once fertile, now arch over
empty spaces, landscapes drawn dry
by the pull of relentless introspection:
how silence folds into itself,
a fabric worn thin at the elbows.

Here, the wrestle with creation
mirrors the cease of waves on a barren shore:
each retreat, a bare clearing in the soul;
each approach, a turmoil reborn—
nature's own breath, in and out,
    a rhythm scored deep in the marrow.

And so, in the gathering shade of twilight,
    where whispers of Goethe and Hölderlin linger,
I find strength in their enduring shadows,
cast long by the low, solemn sun:
the cycles of despair and revelation,
    a quiet close, endless, profound.

Forsaken Hymn no. 310

The empty spaces Archie left behind,
vibrant as the silence after thunder:
 he, too, was a storm, relentless and wild,
his laughter—sharp cracks in the serene sky,
 echoing across the still fields of my mind.
Each memory: a leaf stirred by his winds.

I trace the contours of absence, the way
 night gathers in the corners of a room,
its darkness not just a lack but a shade,
rich and deep, filled with the whispers of trees.
The call of an owl punctuates the dark:
a reminder, life pulses in quiet.

In the aftermath, where silence blooms,
it is not emptiness that fills the air
 but the possibility of new seeds.
This cycle of decay and renewal,
 a constant hum beneath the soil's surface—
we endure, rooted yet always reaching.

Forsaken Hymn no. 311

In the circuit of ancient stones, I tread:
each step a syllable in the long sentence
that began in your mind, cascaded down:
pages that measured the pulse of a city
now pulse beneath my shoes, rhythmic
as the heartbeat of the buried time.

Here, where gulls wheel over the Liffey's rush,
their cries stitching sky to water, echoes
of your narrative weave through the air:
a tapestry visible only to those, like me,
who seek the hidden threads, the latent
messages in the mundane, profound.

Thus, as twilight merges with the streetlamp's glow,
Dublin transforms into a manuscript
that breathes, speaks in your voice:
I listen, learning not just to read, but to hear.
Connected by the continuum of words,
a conversation complete across centuries.

Forsaken Hymn no. 312

In this land where light shifts,
   lives like Archie's flutter:
   brief illuminations in the undergrowth
   of continuous histories.
The ground, a manuscript
scrawled in the ink of shadows:
sunlight writes a fleeting prose

across the open page of noon.
   Beneath these ancient oaks,
whispers linger in the leaves—
the earth, keeping not just seeds
  but the imprints of old souls,
as if stones and soil remember

each footstep that once danced
or marched upon their backs,
bearing ghosts and glory alike.
   And here I stand, pondering
the duality of moment and memory:

Forsaken Hymn no. 313

Vast green sweeps: Ireland's eyes coolly staring,
the weave of cloud and light, dim pathways: my steps
led not here by choice but by winds—unseen forces,
like spores drifting silently across seas and stories,
unmoored: here where dreams ache in their deep hold,
 shadowed by the vast, indifferent sky's lean.

 These rented rooms echo with the currency of solitude,
a coin flipping—heads then tails—chance's cruel game,
a murmur of fate, laughed at by gods, if gods there be
who watch o'er human fragiles, ever bound to trial,
each breath a wave, my pulse the tide's gentle push
 against the shoreless moments of this strained exile.

Now, as I lay, the dusk gathers its cool silks around me,
threadbare but mine to claim: I sift through this strange peace,
 whispering to each star pinned sharp against the night,
canvas of the cosmos, teaching resilience, broad sweeps
 of a painter's brush: life's textures, rich and wanting,
all paths leading not home, but to the heart's quiet rest.

Forsaken Hymn no. 314

Chill air, like tendrils, fingers under:
night's cloak pulls tight, never sunder.
Moon, a frail beacon, guides on stone
where hooves trace murmurs, silent drone:
hopes and fears, specters at my side,
lost less in path than in the ride.

Echoes of a myth, worn thin
whispering stories woven into skin,
The fabric of her green, so slight,
yet heavy with the tales of knight
and dragon, laid in peace or strife,
   weaving through the weave of life.

In our mingling voices, rise
songs born from earth, stretch to the skies,
shadow and light in tender war,
not one without the other for:
in our journey's quiet close,
each step finds peace where trust grows.

Forsaken Hymn no. 315

Beneath the echoes of ancient cries, the soil:
singed yet singing a soft, nascent tune,
roots whispering in hushed dialects of renewal:
how growth emerges from the shadow of doom.
Each blackened blade of grass, a testament:
robust in its frailty, courage threaded thin,
reaching upward, as if to test the temperament

   of skies, questioning what falls from within.
   And here, amidst the aftermath, stand I:
    pondering the dragon's breath, now a gentle sigh,
the sword's weight a lingering question, why
the cycle spins: from ash to birth, under the same sky.
Steady, the pulse of new beginnings swells:

the breeze shifts, carrying both seed and spell,
the landscape—a canvas, painting tales of fell
and risen, whispers of what time will never quell.
   I lower my blade, the tool of both defend and rend,
feeling roots tug at my boots, drawing me to blend
with this transformed earth, where dark and light amend:

Forsaken Hymn no. 316

In the glow of half-lit thought, I wonder:
is there order in chaos, precision in the wind
that scatters leaves helter-skelter down the path,
or in the stars' cold gleaming, vast and aloof,
do they follow a script, unseen, yet strict,
as loomed by the hands of a cosmic weaver?

    The dance of a peach, tossed, not thrown,
in jest, a moment's mirth unwrapping
dark litigations of belief: every act,
however small, charged with the energy
of unseen particles, colliding in silence,
a physics of fate, unwritten, yet unfolding.

And I recall, mother—her laughter, storming,
    no less real for its suddenness, its evanescence—
how life itself is a series of such bursts:
joyous, then calm, then turbulent once more.
We stand, minute and mighty, beneath skies,
    learning to read the weather of our souls.

Forsaken Hymn no. 317

In the churn of daily grind, my hands:
weathered by the gales, stitch by stitch—
binding elements: sea, wind, earth, and fire.
The horizon teems with half-sung tales
of early departures and late returns,
each wave a brittle page in the vast diary.

Moments scatter like seeds on this wild soil,
connections rooted deep as ancient oaks;
Dr. Zimmerman's promise: a leaf budding out
in the cold snap, a quiet testament
to the enduring cycles of renewal;
    life pulses, even in the thickest ice.

Under stars, our paths weave and warp,
intertwined by threads invisible:
each decision a pebble rippling outward.
My wife, the nurturer, tends her garden,
each bloom an echo of our entwined hearts—
and here, grounded, I find my lasting tether.

Forsaken Hymn no. 318

In the quiet room, thoughts echo:
    each a leaf fallen on still water,
rippling outward, where the hardness
of loss softens in the lapse of time:
the leg, once a pillar, now a memory crackling
like dry leaves underfoot.

How strange it is, the body's accounting,
subtracting flesh to sum a spirit,
Archie's shadow dances on the walls:
a specter in the half-light, halved yet whole,
where pain transmutes to something golden,
    precise as the physics of decay.

The specter and man, twined in this dance,
the mind's eye reconstructs wholeness
from shards: not just loss but transformation,
    a reassembling in the echoes of heartbeat—
a continuance faithful as the dawn:
    life asserts, insists, endures, even fragmented.

Forsaken Hymn no. 319

I weave through the waning moonlight,
   each step a soft thud on the cold path:
   every echo, a fragment of history,
undulating into the vast canvas of night.
The leaves rustle: a symphony in the breeze,
    their whispers, like the chatter of atoms,
bouncing off each other in the silence,

   a delicate dance of organic equations.
   Beneath my feet, the earth tells tales
of seeds that once clung to these soils,
roots entangled in a silent struggle:
life pushing through, relentless and fierce.
    In this quiet, I find the rhythm of existence,

   the pendulum swing from seed to dust,
a never-ending loop, stitched with time's
   fine thread: it holds, it tethers, it binds.
As the stars wheel overhead, indifferent,
their cold light a balm to my thoughts,
the universe expands with each breath:

Forsaken Hymn no. 320

Among these ancient stones and newer roads:
the falcon soars above, old cliffs below—
a cycle: eternal, unwinding threads,
the pulse of earth that beats where no one sees.
  Below, fungi lace through soil, root to tree,
    speaking in chemicals: a coded dance.
Here, history whispers through the leaves:

    Pearse's freedom, a mixed inheritance.
  The land, worn by the shoes of many pilgrims,
holding tight to tales of rebel songs,
as though the past might bloom into the present,
and change might write the wrongs.
  But still the buses run their steadfast courses,
paths unchanged by the weight of fallen statues.

Each wheel turn a murmur against stasis,
    yet, in their rounds, an echo of the static.
  The modern mixes with the old in whispers:
    nature's truth, beneath the city's crust.
What is freedom but the chance to witness
seasons change, as all things must?

Forsaken Hymn no. 321

  In the silence of the chapel:
where light filters through stained glass,
casting mosaics of sea-dawn on cold stone,
    I kneel, soaked in the hues of heritage,
    where prayers once soared
and my mother's whispers resonate still.

I pass the cookie, simple,
laden with the weight of unvoiced histories,
her spectral hands guiding mine unseen:
this small sacrament, a confluence
    of past aspirations, spectral and worldly,
where dreams echo against realities.

In this offering, connections weave,
small acts expanding into cosmic tales,
each crumb a star in the broader night,
trails not of failure but pathways
undrawn yet deeply felt:
a circle complete, hands clasped in silent acknowledgment.

Forsaken Hymn no. 322

Beneath the whisper of leaves: the slow,
steady drip of time's unending tap,
its rhythm scribed in the cool breath of evening,
each drop a note in the quiet symphony
  of thoughts, where Churchill walked,
his shadow mingling with Archie's ephemeral stride.

Both men, like trees in a dense forest,
stood rooted in the fertile soils of adversity:
from the dark, they cultivated light,
their lives a lattice of leaves and light,
and I, listening to the murmur of the wind,
find solace in the architecture of their resolve.

  The twilight deepens, bringing the promise
of a night filled with the stir of stars,
  each one a story, a sparkle of the perpetual,
and here, in the embrace of impending darkness,
  I sit, pen in hand, inspired by the legacy
that binds us in an unbreakable weave of continuance.

Forsaken Hymn no. 323

Mist wraps the earth in early light,
  its cool breath mingling with dawn's keen
whisper: such are the moments that compose
  the vastness of a single, fleeting day.
Each leaf, each droplet of dew:
an intricate universe, vast within its smallness,
  hovering at the edge of perception,

as transient as the lifespans we measure
in heartbeats against the eternal pulse
of a cosmos indifferent to our joys and despair.
  We tread upon the soft carpet of fallen leaves,
a mosaic wrought by time's patient hands,
decaying into the fertile silence:

this is the humus of generations,
nurturing the roots of tomorrow's forests,
  where new growth whispers of old truths.
  Such cycles, marked by the arching sun,
guide me to ponder the imprints left
  by those who walked these paths before:

Forsaken Hymn no. 324

Where once laughter tangled with dawn's
　early light: the empty lot spreads,
open and unyielding: an expanse
echoing absences: how the robin
still seeks the vanished feeders:
how roots probe, blind and undirected:
　　beneath, where worms tunnel

　faithfully through the silent, dark earth:
a testament to cycles, to the relentless
urge of life pressing through decay:
even as we linger in the afterglow
of what was: the heart weighs
the delicate balance of dust to dust:
each memory sifting through fingers,

leaving behind the grit of reality:
and yet, through the thin veils
of mourning, the world whispers,
　insists on the interminable passage:
days into years, grief into gradual
acceptance: at last, we learn:

Forsaken Hymn no. 325

In the small hours, asymmetry rules:
    my body a map of discordant zones,
right foot cold, left knee warm,
a testament to the unevenness of life,
each limb declaring its own climate,
seeking comfort from its pair.

Skin against the age-worn fabric whispers,
shifting, restless from the staleness
of hours too still, too long:
the night rearranges, thoughts clear
as the fabric of dreams dissolves,
    leaving raw the edges of waking life.

Guarded, yet open like the sky at dawn,
    I am fortress and fugitive,
    my vulnerabilities huddled close,
knee under chin, a silent shield;
each breath a subtle defiance,
finding peace in the pulse of persistence.

Forsaken Hymn no. 326

Through thickets of psyche and symbol: here,
beneath layers of Freud's ancient texts,
unfold vast fields of thought unbounded:
beyond the primal screams and infant cries
    that populate his charted terrains:
a canvas stretched, vast as starlit skies.

In dreams, our quiet depths speak, articulate
the complex whispers of wind through grass,
    echo patterns not scripted by past traumas
but by currents of thought, sweeping,
unfettered by the hands of paternal doctrines:
the mind's river carving its own course.

    And so beneath the stern gaze of tradition
I find a resilience, an ecological vastness,
    where each idea buds, grows, connects,
interlinked like neurons sparking life:
our truths not fixed, but fluid, like water—
    a stream flowing onward, to an open sea.

Forsaken Hymn no. 327

Leaf whispers catch the salt breeze:
unruly tales spun by the sea,
its rhythms charting paths in sands,
not one wave cresting like another:
nature's own script, never still,
a flux of constant revision.

Each gull's flight, a slice through skies,
mirroring my pen's arc on paper,
both scribing—air, earth—indifferent yet intimate,
connected in the swirl of creation
where thoughts grow wild as weeds,
each bloom a silent testament.

As hours dissolve into the rhythm of tides,
my thoughts turn: the vast mechanics of night
begin their celestial course
and under stars, I grasp at the tangible
only to find all is transient—though,
by the sea, I am ever returning home.

Forsaken Hymn no. 328

In the fold of a leaf: the order: chaos:
  life's contrasts bend, the mechanics of breath,
each inhale a vast expanse, each exhale
    a retreat to minuscule complexities:
the leaf is a universe, its veins roads
to myriad destinies, mapped yet unknown.

Atoms dance: the buzz, the whirl of it all:
ephemeral yet eternal, the pulse
    of quantum strings strumming beneath the sheen
  of a mundane drip of morning dew,
each droplet reflecting not just light,
but the enigma of being here, there.

In the weave of it all, the tight, the loose:
patterns emerge, retreat, in the fabric
of reality where threads pull or fray:
and so, through the chaotic weave I find
a semblance of order, a hint that binds:
all ends, continuous, none truly stray.

Forsaken Hymn no. 329

The sea speaks in currents deep and wide:
its whispers carry truths old as light
that dance at the intersection where
    waves kiss land, retreat, then surge again
like memories in the mind's quiet dusk—
a perpetual ebb, flow, and echo.

Beneath my feet, sand shifts, impermanent,
counting each moment in grains so slight
as to laugh at the span of human plans,
mapping a brief trail in the winds of time
    before waves reclaim what they had lent:
the shore's soft ledger of existence.

And in this space, the surf's constant hum
reminds me: change is the only true constant,
our lives but whispers against the vast
    chorus of nature's unfaltering song.
    Here, standing small, embraced by the breeze,
I find peace in the grandeur of the simple.

Forsaken Hymn no. 330

In this cold field: history whispers,
   winds carry the weight of memories,
caressing the ancient stones
where names barely cling: erosion's slow kiss,
   each groove a testament, not just of past lives,
but of the persistence of stone.
The young woman by the graveside, deliberate,
   fingers tracing air like art,

pauses: what does she summon
in the quiet hum of the Irish dusk?
Is it the murmur of life or the silence
of those who danced here before?
It's curious, this blend of stone and breath,
   how the legacies intertwine:
     Yeats might say we step through, not to,
    the vibrant field blooms not just with flowers,

but with echoes: each petal a story,
each root an anchor deep in the loam.
    And so, I wander, not lost but threading,
through the living tapestry,
seeking my echo in the weave,
   hoping to leave a mark, soft yet indelible,
    on the grand continuum:

Forsaken Hymn no. 331

Packing slips between thoughts: leaves rustle
in the wind: science, too, claims nothing stays:
entropy moves toward dispersion, not order:
Each book a sediment of my past,
the heft of paper, the splice of ink,
map the topography of my years, unbound.
Time folds on itself like well-worn clothes,

crushed into corners of the same old trunk:
how many departures make a home?
The sea, a vast loop that returns always
   to the place of leaving: a mirror
reflecting back my deeper stirrings:

This roaming, an orbit around an unseen core,
   connections spun, fragile as spider silk—
Yvette's laugh, the scholar's gaze, briefly held.
   Yet in transit, the heart thrums a truth:
infinite expanses cradle our brief encounters,
moments that pulse, then dissolve.

Forsaken Hymn no. 332

In the first light, dew reflects infinity:
a universe held in a single drop,
    each leaf a testament to transience,
each fallen petal underscored by time.
The chorus rises as day expands:
wind's whisper through the towering oaks,
    narration in the rustle, an echo of soft truths,

the footprints of the sun in shifting sands.
Every moment pulses with the life of stars,
the swirling dance of atoms, unseen,
yet felt in the breeze that charts its course
through the open heart of the sky.
    The geometry of existence, fractal and fleeting,
hipped in the design of petals and waves,

    where melodies play the chords of change,
resonating deeply within the porous earth.
    In this cycle, where endings blend into beginnings,
we find the threads of continuous creation:
our voices part of the symphony, notes
rising and falling, in perfect, ephemeral harmony.

Forsaken Hymn no. 333

In Ballsbridge, silence wraps its arms:
the air, thick with yesteryear's pain,
   cradles a city's heartbreak as I stand,
contemplating how roots intertwine,
grow deep, like the sorrow embedded
in this soil: the world's grave commonplace.

A fly, fragile harbinger, buzzing
briefly by, carries the weight of history
in its tiny wings: does it feel the pulse
of the lost, like I do? Or does it glide
unswervingly on, destined to witness
the sorrow of others from afar?

   I reach towards the end of this remembrance,
wondering if, like me, Yeats ever sensed
the sharp sting of reality in his bones,
   or if his thoughts, like leaves in the wind,
escaped the gravity of flesh and blood—
so we continue, circling back to where we start.

Forsaken Hymn no. 334

the cosmos pens us into being, draws us
into the margins of a vast page, blots of ink:
    we expand, diffuse, yet cling to the notion:
      life, a line traced between birth and that silence,
which like a dark river runs parallel to our days,
unseen, sensed, a chill that beckons:

does the leaf understand the fall?
or the river the ocean it rushes toward?
each drop melds, loses itself in the larger body:
so we, particles in a grand sweep of unknowing,
try to embrace the whispers of space,
the molecular symphony playing within us:

and yet, I seek a key, one not to unlock
    but to wind back, to understand the mechanism
of cessation, the unwritten rule of an ending,
guided by the light of stars burned out long ago,
    each a beacon in the vast, indifferent dark,
      pointing us toward acceptance, toward peace.

Forsaken Hymn no. 335

The leaf's spin mirrors my own: how it falls,
twisting in the unforeseen currents of air,
akin to decisions that swirl, clouded,
    above the gravity of grounding needs:
balances tipped by the weight of a breath,
the fall a slow dance guided by winds of change.

Responsibility: an ocean vast,
its tides pull with quiet insistence,
the natural laws of give and take
    etched deep in the furrows of my brow—
each crest, a crisis; each trough, a lull:
restless, the ceaseless cycle turns.

In the stillness between gusts, clarity:
    a knowing that fairness is not merely
numbers aligned but lives intertwined.
Thus, I stand, a steward of more than stone,
holding firm to empathy as my standard,
final faith in our collective flowering.

Forsaken Hymn no. 336

In dim lit halls of mind's own make:
thoughts tread softly on old tracks,
each print a memory, echo of a touch.
A fabric, finely woven, $200 worth,
feels less than the warmth it covers,
cold cash against the skin's honest heat.

The science of desire maps our wants
like stars charted in clear night skies:
each point a burning mass, a greedy pull.
    Grasping at the past, palms open,
we reach for ghosts, clad in luxury,
    forgetting the earth beneath bare feet.

Yet, how simple joys unfold, petal-like,
in the presence of a long-lost love—
her hand clasping his, orbits aligned.
    I stand, relearning the texture of time,
witness to the gravity we craft:
every farewell a small death, every hello a rebirth.

Forsaken Hymn no. 337

Sculpted arches: continuity in stone,
the pulse of time carved deep in ancient grain:
our hands trace where old hands once set their own,
a dialogue through centuries maintained.
Under the echo of their lasting craft,
voices blend: the stonecutter, the mystic.
What permanence in fragile human paths,

ephemeral lives pressed into the cryptic
richness of the earth, our stories told
in whispers, layering like sediment:
layers, hard and brittle, yet bold,
a substratum of mingled intent.
An archway stands, defying transience,
threshold to the temple of existence.

Each crossing a pilgrimage of sorts:
from known to unknown, shadow into light.
In this doorway, time is a cohort
inviting reflections, subtle and slight.
Thus, we are all travelers, history's thread
woven, remembered—here, this moment's head.

Forsaken Hymn no. 338

In the morning's sharp embrace, the day begins:
    its first light splits the horizon, where sea meets sky,
tinted by the bright colors of the flag, snapping,
asserting its presence against the quiet dawn,
and I, standing witness, feel a pulse connect—
earth to sky, nation to soul, a singular thread.

That thread weaves through the cold, expansive air,
connecting moments of clarity to the jumbled
corners of diplomacy: how similar it is—
to the wind's craft at sea, unseen yet palpable;
    it sculpts the waves, directs the drifting gulls,
a force felt more in effect than in visibility.

Concluding, where threads of thought and breeze unite,
    the fabric of identity and place is cast,
spun from the looms of natural order and chaos.
As the door swings open, as if by design or neglect,
    freedoms echo in the wild calls of gulls:
each cry a note in the symphony of being.

Forsaken Hymn no. 339

In this autumn of my life, half-shed
leaves, I pause: the forest breathes in its
   cyclical sighs, whispering through branches:
  each leaf a story caught mid-fall,
    hanging, each a testament of survival
in the quiet dusk of the year.

Change is neither friend nor adversary:
it is the pulse beneath the bark, the unseen
   force pushing the roots deeper into
earth: here, in these depths, my past,
my decisions, my forgotten selves intertwine
   with the mineral nourishment of acceptance.

The landscape shifts: mountains erode,
  rivers find new paths to the sea,
   and I, too, find myself reshaped:
a sculpture worn by the winds of time,
my edges smoothed by the gentle abrasion
of days: thus ends my pondering, at peace.

Forsaken Hymn no. 340

In the span of parchment, age-yellowed and crisp,
I seek: not just contours, but the essence
of monastic echoes, stilled lives nestled
    in the tight folds—where ink runs as rivers do:
veined, deep, pulsing with a history
    that binds more than splits.

Maps: they are promises, myths told
in whispers of scale and legend, a cartographer's
    dream that landscapes can be tamed,
mind-marked in meshed lines: how I wander
amidst the slated ruins, my fingers tracing
each boundary that once held a prayer.

    Thought pivots on the axis of what's lost
and gained in the reading: this map, a gift
intended to chart paths, not stir souls—
yet here I am, caught in the spiritual cartography
where every line invites deeper pilgrimage,
a quiet reckoning with the etched contours of being.

Forsaken Hymn no. 341

In the silence between stars, a dialogue:
cosmic dust transmitting tales through voids,
   each particle a letter sealed in dark
energies, traveling vast spans of space,
forming bonds unseen but deeply felt:
this is how roots speak to raining sky.
Curving back, like light around a black hole,

thoughts orbit the nucleus of self,
each revolution drawing tighter circles,
deepening the gravity of knowing.
Leaves whisper my fame to the wind:
   should I listen, or should I speak back,
pondering how my echo shapes the air,
the air that sustains mountains, rivers,

and the small unseen creatures below?
Cycles close as closure comes in whispers,
like breath that fogs a mirror, then clears,
revealing the interconnected mesh—
my name, once etched in solitude,
   now shared, reformed in countless minds,
concluding not in fame but in connection.

Forsaken Hymn no. 342

In the crease of an old resume,
   a spill of ink bleeds more than black:
memories, pooling at the edges—
   each drop a mirror, reflecting fragments
   of days consumed by the fire
   of relentless passing time.

In the marrow—the tender echos:
not of accolades, but of laughter
shared in stolen moments under stars,
the soft whisper of grass beneath feet
bare, like secrets traded between old friends,
or lovers intertwined beneath the moon.

What remains in the end:
not the lines that have been written,
but those left dancing on the verge of ink,
unspoken yet vibrating within the heart's deep well.
   Closed books tell no tales of lives truly lived—
only the silent acknowledgment of paths tread silently.

Forsaken Hymn no. 343

Beneath the elms: their branches' span
like neurons firing in the dusk,
relay the whispers of the park:
how life converges, breaks, flows on.
A leaf detaches, spirals down—
    a slow descent through still-warm air,
mimicking the fall of man:

from vibrancy to still decay.
Yet children laugh, their bright voices
crack the shell of my reserve;
dogs chase, unabashed by age,
while ducks glide by, serene, detached.
    Loneliness: the shared human lot—
each soul's path winds apart, entwines:

I ponder this, as shadows stretch,
marking time with darkening lines.
    But see how sunlight filters through
the leaves, a benediction mild,
casting nets of golden peace
where sorrow meets the edge of joy.

Forsaken Hymn no. 344

Beneath the surface of punitive gestures,
   a simple leaf unfolds in morning light:
    each vein a narrative of nutrients,
drawn from the depths where dark meets moisture.
So too justice, rooted in darker soils,
grows visible only when the time commands.

The tree stands firm: structure, function in one,
   a living testament to steady growth,
even as its leaves face the autumn's purge.
And aren't we much like this arboreal plight?—
   shedding parts, a cyclical renewal
to balance on the tightrope of existence.

Yet, in the quiet decay of fallen leaves,
   the forest floor composes symphonies
of interconnections: decay breeds life.
   So must our understanding shift and fall,
   allowing new truths to worm through old soil,
and from such humus, wisdom might then bloom.

Forsaken Hymn no. 345

The river unfurls, a steady pulse:
lifeblood of earth, current's caress
marks time not in hours but by the silvery
scales of a salmon: sleek, rippling,
caught in the tug of relentless flow,
bearing the burden of freedom.

Along these banks, wealth whispers in the reeds:
Archie, with pockets deep, his laughter hollow,
gazes into the current, seeking perhaps
   some gleam of truth in its depths,
the way light fractures on the riverbed,
broken by water, yet somehow whole.

For what are we if not seekers, the line
cast again in hope of connection—
   the brief flash beneath surface tensions,
a mutual struggle within grasp's reach?
This river, bearer of tales,
ends: acknowledging the cycles we trace.

Forsaken Hymn no. 346

The cycle turns, relentless: a leaf crackles,
fallen, not far from the branch it knew as home,
   its green vigor spent: does it sense its fade
to compost, even as it feeds the soil?
Decay: but a pause in sentences
of growth: each molecule recomposing,
ready to be called back into the congress
of roots: thus, the eternal dialogues of earth.

   Atoms exchange in quiet fervor, no less
fierce for their subtlety: a flower's bloom
   torqued by the helix of DNA,
its code dictating petals' spread and hue.
   Underneath, worms till the dark with purpose,
blind to the sun's arc yet crucial to its energy,
their castings a testament to cycles unseen,

   silent laborers in the grand symphony.
   And here I stand, leaf-like, in this expanse
of evolving stories: each breath a bridge,
each moment a stir in the great whirl
of being and unbeing, sowing seeds
of thought that might, just might, blossom
into understanding: the beauty of the cycle closes.

Forsaken Hymn no. 347

Leaves gather, silent witnesses:
each serrated edge, a story suppressed,
fallen into the obscure depths
where water holds the echoes
of sin, scandal: refracted,
distorting like memory.

This pond: a lens capturing
the world's relentless churn,
Marylou's face ripples across
time's surface, caught between
 judgment and sorrow,
her tale, a stone thrown.

In these still waters,
a quiet reflection of turmoil:
 how we sensationalize, then seek
redemption, as if the cycle
could cleanse the deeds.
In the end, nature absorbs it all.

Forsaken Hymn no. 348

In the vastness, where stone whispers to wind:
each grain of sand, a star in its own firmament,
   paths spiral like galaxies, pulling inward:
my thoughts orbit around the silent breath
  of earth, unfolding like the lotus at dawn,
   shedding night's shadow as light edges the petals.

  Each moment, balanced precariously on the tip
of existence, a dance of light and darkness:
the rustle of leaves, a symphony in the quiet,
speaking the language of the unsaid,
   where roots clutch deep in the dark soil,
tethering the transient to the eternal pulse.

Here, amid the ceaseless turn of the world,
  I find stillness within the storm,
   a heart centered by the spiral's calm eye:
all paths converge, entwined by the journey,
   life's intricate embroidery—vivid and fleeting,
   a resolute whisper: I am here, in the forever now.

Forsaken Hymn no. 349

We bend with time: the weight of years
    folds us, origami-like, into shapes
of who we were, who we will be:
the fading jest of youth's bright laughter
stills to the deeper timbre of the sage,
    edges blurring in the twilight haze.

  The constant flow of tides erases
footprints left where once we danced,
a beach now smoothed by waves of change:
ephemeral as the daily news,
yet inscribed in memory's fragile bones:
    this shift, the soft attrition of the self.

  Here, beneath the vast, indifferent sky,
I trace the arc of our collective journey,
not marked by loud proclamations
    but by silent, nurturing adaptations,
each wave receding but leaving behind
    the richness of ripened understanding.

Forsaken Hymn no. 350

The mind's eye, never still, surveys the room:
literary spirits mix with the actual,
each sip a deep dive into narrative's pool,
where lessons bubble up, accidental.
Pages rustle like leaves in a soft gale,
a dance of intellect amid the drifts
    of thought: here a clear trail, there a veil,
each turn a story, each shift a gift.

    Through the window, light sieves through glass,
   fragments of a world aglow, offering
itself, unmasked: how quickly hours pass,
yet slow each photon's timeless wandering.
Reflections on the glass, or in the mind?
Blurred lines where self and shadows blend,

confusing the memories we find
with those we invent, craft, and then defend.
In solitude, this quiet alchemy
transforms mundane to profound: a quest
for deeper truths beneath the frothy sea
    of surface thoughts that never rest.

Forsaken Hymn no. 351

Among weathered stones and moss, thoughts drift:
  like debris caught in the old mill's spin,
water flows, relentless, shaping granite
  and hours spent away from the pull
of routine's tight weave: mundane threads
    shed beneath the sky's wide blue thinking.

Gristmill's grind, a backdrop hum to ponder—
  forces: natural, human, intertwining,
each grain broken open like a secret
held inside the earth's hard fist,
opening to the philosophy of soil:
every end a passage to beginning.

  In this space, where blades cut air with ease,
my spirit, unbound, sings of roots,
reaching deep where dark nurtures whispers.
Here stands the soul's true terrain, free—
where past chases present into future,
  and a bird's song completes the circle.

Forsaken Hymn no. 352

In the shadow of these ancient griefs,
our echoes weave: Armenian whispers,
Jewish sighs, Ibo cries: strung through
the corridors of cruel history: all
stitched into humanity's frayed tapestry:
the cycle spins from dark to light:

and Archie, eyes haunted like hollow stars,
  speaks of culture as transient smoke:
a flicker through the ages, brief and bright,
turning solid wood to spectral ash:
each transformation: a betrayal or a redemption,
every spark: a potential for renewal:

    so here I stand, pondering the balance
between loss and the hope it seeds:
the world's wounds: deep yet not destined
  to forever bleed, for within each scar's sharp sting
lies the gentle power of understanding—
a closing chord that resonates with peace.

Forsaken Hymn no. 353

    beneath our feet: the layered earth speaks
of cycles: sediment to sediment,
      leaf falls, decays, and from its fabric
    the soil nurses the oak, robust and branching.
     inside this canopy, we plumb the depths
  of time: a fossil encased in stone,
a glimpse of life solidified,

    capturing a creature's last breath on a lake's edge,
a narrative sealed beneath layers: the slow,
     pressing dance of the geological,
constantly rewriting itself: each era
a page in earth's dense, unread manuscript.
    but we, gathering knowledge: pour over
maps, old texts, spectral data, seeking

to understand not just the how
but the why: from cosmos to the quantum field,
where particles flicker with possibilities,
briefly aligning like stars, then dispersing
     into chaos—a pattern we chase,
until, at last, we rest, knowing the world continues.

Forsaken Hymn no. 354

Line by line, thought weaves:
each strand pulling closer the night's chill,
the stars blink: indifferent spectators
in the vast cosmic play where love
scripts its tumultuous scenes,
binding particles, waves: interlaced fates.

Moonlight casts long shadows,
   the stage set in silvers and blues:
atoms dance to the subtle rhythms of chance,
   drawn out by the gravity of each fleeting glance.
How molecules assemble,
sync to the pulses of our hearts.

And so, we drift: caught in the ebb
   of tides that shaped the shores of our being,
finding in each crest and fall
a mirror of our own undulating desires,
   until in the quiet after, we settle,
softly, into the sands of ourselves.

Forsaken Hymn no. 355

Twilight dapples the window's blush:
tears and twilight, a mix,
each reflection a flux, a fusion
    where vision stirs deep in shifting hues,
and I, tracing lines of worn faces,
        notice: the chill glass doesn't flinch.

This pane separates, yet showcases:
a boundary between the echoed inner,
the call of the evening's cool expanse;
outside, an orb spider spins afresh—
resilient threads glisten,
clinging to dew, to the chance of dawn.

    How much like the web am I?
        Quivering with each breeze, each tremor—
anchored, though seeming adrift,
suspended by strands of past and potential,
        and in the closing of another year:
realize, there is rebirth in the ruins.

Forsaken Hymn no. 356

In the sway of the porch swing, time slows:
its creak a gentle lecture on persistence,
  a symphony played on rusty hinges,
each note a memory, labor's echo.
    Hands, weathered as the wood under my grip,
    speak in splinters of effort and age,
      telling of soil: turned, revered, sown,

    and the seeds—minute, yet bound to burst.
How Archie admired the straight beam,
the unyielding plane, his square true;
each nail a commitment, hammered deep,
    connecting stories, layer by layer.
Beneath this sun-aged canopy, the ghost

of Archie's eye twinkles in the glass,
reflecting dreams priced by roughened palms,
and quiet smiles for small victories.
This house—our stage—stands firm,
      its foundation a testament to the unseen,
    love's labor piled high like seasoned firewood,
ready to ignite on the darkest nights.

Forsaken Hymn no. 357

The weight of whispers: how they linger,
like dust motes caught in a shaft of moonlight,
each speck a soliloquy of loss and longing,
the air thick with the breath of old stories.
   I sift through them, each syllable
     a pulse within the veins of the night:
how one holds another's grief

as a stone cradled in riverbeds,
    smoothed by the relentless flow
of water: always moving, never still.
And in this darkness, where shadows
play the endless game of truth and dare,
I trace the contours of shared heartaches,
   the outline of faces I have never seen

yet know as intimately as my own.
   Imagining their lives, their battles,
    a tapestry woven with the threads
of my own silent meditations.
  The dawn, when it breaks, finds me
    still entwined in these threads,
seeking solace in the symmetry of suffering.

Forsaken Hymn no. 358

The night air carries whispers,
The leaves murmur of change:
   All is flux, motion; yet, we cling
To moments as if they might sustain
Our fragile, fleeting frames
In patterns familiar and tame.

I ponder the permanence of stars,
   Their ancient light piercing time:
A guide for voyagers long since gone,
Their journeys etched in cosmic rhyme.
The universe spins, indifferent to losses
Or the counting of our days and crosses.

In the embrace of shadow, I find grace—
The quiet end to relentless pursuits,
Where memories dissolve in the dark,
Melting the hard residues of pain.
Thus, Archie wanders not in vain;
   Night's end reveals the new day's spark.

Forsaken Hymn no. 359

The sky: a scroll unrolled, bearing light,
its hues bending into the crease of dawn:
each morning, a soft whisper of blue
  tinged with the blush of nascent flame,
marries the chill sea to the warming earth,
binding day to night: a continuous thread.

  The sands, fine and numerous, shift
    underfoot, hinting at the impermanence
of things we deem solid: even mountains,
    once upheaved, wear down to grains,
      every stone a slow, deliberate journey
toward becoming beach: a testimony.

And we, standing at the shore of existence,
    draw lines in the passing: temporary marks,
watch as waves reclaim all efforts:
yet, is there not beauty in the erosion,
in the give and take, the relational dance?
This the cosmos whispers: we are together.

Forsaken Hymn no. 360

The sea recoils, then heaves forward:
    each wave a slow inhale or a surge
that erases footprints as though history
    could be wiped, merged with the currents,
    each crest: a salty testament
    to cycles that pulse beneath our feet.

Tangled in the kelp, the brine, driftwood
arrives, harried by the storm's whim:
carried across waters, journeys not chosen
    but thrust upon the broad backs
of unforgiving waves: particles, intricate
    as the narratives we weave and believe.

  On the shore, footsteps sink, temporary
as the men who once sailed towards horizons
with hearts heavy as the ships that bore them,
    each imprint a relic, stirring dust
    and memory: how we echo, resonate
    through the mists of time, whispering closure.

Forsaken Hymn no. 361

The corridors stretch: endless thoughts,
conjoined like roots under fertile soil,
  each turn a discovery: a new bud
on the seasoned branch of our discourse;
your ideas, spry, entwine with my weathered musings,
    binding us in a loop, a thread spun fine.

This labyrinth of intellect and emotion—
our sanctuary, where echoes shape
the chambers with the weight of words not said;
here, pathways fork, under the watch
of aged ivy-clad walls, that murmured wisdom
with each leaf stirred by the breath of inquiry.

And at the journey's end, a clearing:
a tranquil place where the song,
threaded through generations, finds a note
that holds—luminous and full. The melody
blends our voices, a harmony rich and exact,
    a shared resonance that completes the circle.

Forsaken Hymn no. 362

At the edge of the field, wildflowers bend:
their stems arc with the weight of dew,
captives to the morning's fresh scent,
and the sky stretches wide: a clear blue,
mirroring possibilities or questions
long mused over by wind-tossed grass.

Below, roots tangle in dark communion,
    spreading threads beneath the earth: firm,
silent, yet speaking in nutrient diffusion,
a constant mingle, exchange, and affirm.
Above, leaves flicker in synaptic sunlight,
translating light to sugar: life's quiet triumph.

Then evening pulls the sun under its wing,
    darker blue, as stars wheel and pin the sky:
each a focal point in the vast patterning
of galaxies, each whispering how and why.
    In this stretched canvas, all is interwoven,
and from the vast, we learn: nothing is cloven.

Forsaken Hymn no. 363

In the quiet aisles, silence speaks:
   the dust, a testament to the unseen,
   threads of thought not followed, paths
left untrodden in the vast halls of learning;
yet between the gaps: enlightenment.
I hold a page, feel its pulse,
wonder at the science of missing spaces,
the ecology of the unread,

where ideas, like spores, disperse
   unnoticed, yet grow unseen, critical in the dark.
   Rooted in absence, my knowledge expands
in understanding what I do not know:
   each unturned page a window
to the boundless landscapes of the intellect,
a breeze through an open frame,

inviting the unexplored, completing the circuit.
   In the quiet libraries where whispers linger:
   the echo of steps, soft as thought, on marble—
I pause among giants, unseen texts that hover
   like specters in the aisles: here lies the frontier
   of my undiscovered, stretching infinite
and precisely to the edge of my knowing.

Forsaken Hymn no. 364

In the half-light of decline, the mind
wrestles with the shadow of time:
   how leaves, brown and crisp,
fall in clocks of decay,
   the tick of nature, incessant,
as it crafts the carpet of past seasons.

The room's corners, dim and stocked
with the sediment of the years,
echo faintly: the murmurs of those
   once close, now voices in the draft,
   a flicker of laughter, a pause
in the sighing wind of days gone by.

Yet, growth: even in the creases
of my well-worn face, the map
of life's relentless pursuit,
   there is a budding, slight and unsure,
in the twilight of years, a new leaf,
a testament to the persistence of spring.

Forsaken Hymn no. 365

In the dim glow of an Irish pub, I find
    myself mingling thoughts:
pale ale reflections on the nature of magnanimity,
how it stretches, elastic between the flickers of waxlight,
variegated as the patrons' chorused hums,
every sip a whisper of paths not taken.

There's warmth here, in the murmurs and the musk,
    where forgiveness feels almost material,
a tangible swath of twilight draped over shoulders,
grains of goodwill sifted through the hourglass—
each moment marking time, a soft sediment:
life lived in the hearty clink of glass to glass.

Odd, how a room can mirror the mind,
    how strangers blend into the backdrop
of my own contended solitude,
the lilac in my grasp a token of transient peace:
nature's fleeting signature on the human contract,
every ending a promise: perennial bloom in fallow soil.

Forsaken Hymn no. 366

The threshold calls: ahead, the unknown glimmers,
behind, the familiar mists pull tenderly:
  each path brimmed with its own resonance
of what may be lost or found in stepping
forward or retreating: how the past anchors,
heavy with the gravity of lived moments,

and yet, how the future floats, a spectrum
  of possibilities undefined, untasted:
  the heart hesitates at the edge, measuring
the quantum of leap it dares against
the span of stillness it can bear:
  caught in the silent dialogue of decision,

amid ilex whispers and magnolia's stand.
  The sea's murmur, a distant chant, calls
to the deepest currents of my spirit,
urging flow where water and life converge:
Here, at nature's precipice of change,
I choose: the path unfolds in steps taken.

Forsaken Hymn no. 367

In this city of shifting sands, where dragons:
coil under broken neon, and phoenixes,
   in their fiery dance, rebirth from old cans—
  worlds collide, nature embraces the frayed ends:
of our certainties, nudging life beyond:
   its prescribed orbits: chaos is the lens.

Species long veiled by the concrete and scorn:
now navigate stars scattered on asphalt,
luminous creatures, both native and foreign,
guide the night: their shimmer, a default:
against the darkness civilization built:
paths flare like synapses, bright and tumult.

Serene amid turmoil, a quiet thought:
perhaps chaos is not misplaced order,
   but an order we've narrowly defined,
caught in our own nets of fear, border
drawn tightly until all that's left is the:
breath of change, urging us to reconsider.

Forsaken Hymn no. 368

In the hush of winter's grip, the ice:
crisp, unyielding, fractal mysteries
beneath the skates—here, where breath
  clouds visions, limits sight to moments now:
    I pivot, steel blades carving arcs—
each slice: a decision, a direction set.

The puck hurtles, a comet: its path
  lined with intentions, gravity's own whim—
I respond, not just react: weave
the tapestry of muscle, sinew pulled taut—
life's unpredictable physics governing
my every dive, twist, desperate save.

And when the game ends, silence:
cold echoes off empty bleachers—
tea cooling slowly between our hands,
moments measured in sips and sighs;
all things pass, seasons, games, the cheers—
  yet in our bones, the ice's lessons live on.

Forsaken Hymn no. 369

As I thread through veils: my consciousness,
a journey inward, deep and boundless,
   each thought a leaf, turned, considered—
so emerges the texture of self,
   the layers: not merely surface, but
deep as roots in fertile darkness.

In the silence, the mind's echoes—
   I consider the body's fragile temple,
subject to unseen tremors, whispers cold,
   the seasonal garb we wear: defenses,
thin against the vast siege of life,
awareness our only steadfast shield.

From this quiet convent of thought,
I gaze outward, the horizon a line
   drawn in shifting sands, constant,
yet ever elusive in its detail—
a testament, perhaps, that in the end,
   we stand, knowing only the bounds of our quest.

Forsaken Hymn no. 370

The rain speaks in a Morse code of solitude:
   its insistent tap at the window, a rhythm
   that sculpts the silence into fragments of thought;
each drop carries a weight, the subtle guilt
of distant days, paths diverged and left unexplored.
   Rain's patter scripts the narrative of water,
   cycle of sky to earth, absorbed and reborn:

such is the movement of our lives, each turn
a mirror to nature's tireless pendulum, shifting
from presence to absence, a dance of shadows
overlapping, yet never fully merging.
Beneath the ceaseless whisper, my heart beats
to the tempo of falling water, questioning

the lines that connect and divide:
how much of me is woven into the lives
I touched, and how much stands alone,
distinct as drops sliding down separate paths?
In this gray solitude, I find the edges of myself,
   and there—amidst the rain's soft sighs—a closure.

Forsaken Hymn no. 371

Each morning breaks over the spine of the hills:
the light drifts, a slow river of gold,
seeping through leaves, stitching shadows
to the fabric of dew-laden grass.
   Here, beneath the vault of waking sky,
she listens: each breath a story, told in silence.

The hound, loyal sentinel, paws softly
beside her, protector in the vastness
of this ungentle wilderness.
Together, navigating through the murmur
and crunch of underbrush: a symphony
played on the bones of the earth.

  In the cool, her thoughts weave through the trees,
patterns of longing and loss, knitted close
as nightfall cloaks their steps.
The promise of return: simple, unfaltering,
  a quiet truth held in the gaze of steady stars,
   the heart's quiet pulse beneath a healing hand.

Forsaken Hymn no. 372

The slow unraveling of seasons: how
each leaf teaches the art of letting go,
   subtly shedding green for gold, a show
of quiet transitions, nature's soft breath
on the pane of time: a whisper, not a heave,
   the steady pulse of earth's heart beneath.

Molecular, those intricate dances
underneath, roots spreading like thoughts,
   deep into the dark richness, sipping
last summer's rain saved in soil's hold:
chemicals exchanging vows, a binding
of life to the ever-evolving planet.

And I, observer of this grand cosmos,
wonder as stars blink the truth in Morse—
   silvery dots spelling out the universe's course—
   how small a part I play in the infinite,
yet how vital the leaf, the root, the dirt:
all cycles close, completing their work.

Forsaken Hymn no. 373

The dusk deepens, and so does my brooding:
   nature's script plays out, predator and prey,
     yet here, I am caught, neither beast nor bounty,
but a thinker bound by the very roots
that grant escape: contemplation, a thread
   spooling through the eye of life's needle.

In the dim glow, shadows stretch long—
the owl, silent, sweeps through the underbrush,
its talons, a harsh decree, clutch tight
   a field mouse in its final squeal:
Is this the cruelty of necessity
   or the necessity of cruelty?

Beneath the calm, unrest stirs: the quiet
   not quiet, the stillness charged.
Every life hung by a thread, heavy with the weight
of survival, where to resist is to exist—
   and in this existential weave, I find
    closure in the continuity of nature's hand.

Forsaken Hymn no. 374

In the measure of light, the shade,
a balance delicate: fractal edges of leaves
cutting wide beams into narrow threads,
intersections where shadow meets glow:
    here, the fabric of existence stretches,
thin, like the membrane of a dragonfly's wing.

    Each pulse in the vein of a leaf,
the slow draw of water from root to tip,
mirrors her silent struggle: growth
against the press of darkness, life
claiming its right under weight,
each breath a defiance of the void.

And so in her words, a resonance
with the rattling whispers of dried leaves:
a harmony in the desolation,
the echo of her spirit in the hollows
    of my quiet room: her courage, a beacon
soft as the dusk, ending the day in peace.

Forsaken Hymn no. 375

In this stretch of calm after festive noise,
stars peek through the bare treetops:
even the cosmos pauses, breathes out,
   relishes the gentle pull of gravity—
  the dance of mass and space that shapes
    our nights and guides lost voyagers.

Moments settled like fine dust on glass,
etching patterns in transient frost—
each flake: a star, the residue of a storm
  in the quiet cold: matter organized,
a universe beneath our fingertips,
whispering the physics of connection.

Here amid the stillness, amidst decay,
the candle flickers—a lone testament,
    mimicking the first morning's radiance,
     its light casting long shadows,
threading through our collected silences,
each flame a story, finished yet unending.

Forsaken Hymn no. 376

Beneath the crust of ancient texts and dust,
the classroom echoes with the ghostly thrust
of voices: Hopkins, Swift, the milkman's cry,
   each bound by threads of unseen alchemy,
their words a lattice, joining star to bone,
unearthing truths to which all flesh is prone.

   In this dim light, where motes of yesterday
dance with the silence in a grave ballet,
my mind traverses galaxies of thought,
a scholar's quest with mystic wonder fraught,
     where language meets the cold, expansive space,
     and life, a fleeting shadow, finds its trace.

   What binds us here, the learned and the lost,
to linger in this spectral, dust-lit frost?
Is it the ceaseless yearning to transcend,
     or merely time's unyielding, quiet bend?
Each soul a note within the infinite,
our ending written by the star's own light.

Forsaken Hymn no. 377

In the churn of Texas Falls, thoughts break:
  crystal shards in relentless drift,
each icy drop a mirror
  to the tumult of being, the raw nerve
  of existence pummeled by time's relentless fist,
echoing Nietzsche's stark dance of despair.

And what of the sun's bold leap across the horizon,
casting long shadows over our intent?
Here, I pondered the dichotomy of giving:
a reluctant hand, ten shillings pressed
into the worn lines of necessity,
  a child's eyes a mirror to my own plight.

In my wind-torn garden, beauty scatters
like leaves and lost songs of spring,
a testament to impermanence.
Each visitation of awe or dread
is a step toward understanding—
this intricate dance with the universe ends.

Forsaken Hymn no. 378

Beneath the storm's crescendo,
theories of rain: each drop, a prism,
breaking light into a spectrum:
how often have we refracted, unknowingly,
through the slant of skewed perceptions,
yet here, tied to the gravity—

of moments that mark as milestones,
    a thunderclap echoes: it is no ordinary
disturbance but a notable shift
    in the dynamics of atmospheric pressure:
    my thoughts, like charged particles,
collide and scatter, seeking ground—

in this Irish solstice, I find not peace,
but a reframing: roots gently lifting
from their old beds to test new soils,
    where the storm's howl dims,
and quiet—in the shy light,
marks the end, yet also a beginning.

Forsaken Hymn no. 379

Leaffall whispers through the slanted sun:
    an integration of decay and bloom,
cycles couched in the twist of DNA,
    spiral promises in chromosomes:
life, a tender balance of elements,
assembled in the dance of time.

  Energies that shift within and without,
patterns set by the moon's persuasive pull,
    gravity: a binding rhetoric
that speaks to apple and orbit alike,
holding everything together, gathered
in the grasp of invisible forces.

Within this contemplation, nature scribes
its script: the constant flux of birth and death,
cells dying while new ones are born:
    a river flowing through the heart of life,
where all paths meet and meld at the delta,
    ending, yet beginning anew.

Forsaken Hymn no. 380

In the primal cold of ancient caves,
the echo of my doubts rings loud:
how scant the comfort of bear-skin
against the vastness of the unknown,
where stone walls absorb each whispered fear
and return them louder, clearer.

Within this cavern, thoughts like stalactites
drip slowly, forming over lifetimes:
    my constructed home—of timber, yes,
     but more of memory, connection,
      the fabric woven by community's hands,
   sheltering as much as wood and stone.

   I write to Archie across wilds,
our souls' yearnings like penned strokes,
  blending dreams of fragile human lines
with the relentless sea's rhythmic pulse,
  a heartbeat grounding my restless spirit,
each wave's retreat a pull back to safe shadows.

Forsaken Hymn no. 381

In this dimmed hall, where whispers swirl,
the dancer bends light, breaks stillness:
   all eyes drawn as she twists, turns—
a shadow against pale grieving faces,
her body a conduit from despair to something:
   fiercely alive, defiantly bright.

Sorrow's weave loosens beneath her feet,
each step a sentence in the language of loss,
echoing 'Give!' and 'Ow!'—strange punctuation
   in the quietude of our mourning hearts;
here movement speaks louder than words,
      a grammar all its own.

And so we learn, watching her spin,
that grief too is a thing with motion,
not just to be endured but danced through,
a pirouette from the edge of night;
each of us, in turn, must find our rhythm
in the spaces where light persists.

Forsaken Hymn no. 382

In this small hour: clarity opens,
  the weave of fabric split by first light:
    silver threads that anchor the cosmic dance,
the rhythms—pulse and pull of tidal forces.
Each day, a testament to the subtle
turn of Earth: the grand gyre maintained
by celestial gravity: how we stand,

unaware yet deeply riveted.
All around, particles drift, suspended
in the air, reflecting solar flares,
and photons dance on the edge of time,
caught halfway between shadow and gleam.
Here in this fracture: the dawning split

between science and the soul: how tender
each conjecture, mapping the heart's held beats
to the vast, expansive universe.
This corner universe: my kiosk, a node
in the network of these wandering atoms,
each soul's trajectory a beautiful
accident, a whisper of the divine.

Forsaken Hymn no. 383

Ephemeral lights flicker: the day's remnants
cling as shadows stretch, reaching back to dusk,
  where moments hang suspended, ripe with the
secret rhythms of turning earth: how soil
shifts, whispering through roots, rock, burrowing
  life, all mingling where your stillness lies.

Solar arcs traced by meticulous spin,
worlds wheel silently above: the cosmos,
    indifferent, marks no single passing, though
your departure carved deep orbits in me,
your gravity still bending my path, this
flight through voids you vacated too soon.

Yet here, in the cool evening's soft closure,
I seek a dialogue with the departed,
an equation to balance loss, legacy—
to unearth the peace that must lie beneath
dense layers of pain, confusion, love: to
let go, finally, beneath stars' watchful eyes.

Forsaken Hymn no. 384

In the soft murmur of the evening breeze,
I note: the firm oak shifts not as we, its leaves
  whispering tales of seasons past: a flux
   in quiet disguise, gathering the dusk
   into its aged limbs: how youth and its wants
flee, quicksilver, through fingers, teach us haunts
  of memory like lessons of the sky—

each cloud a passage, shaped, unheld, drifting by:
we are such vapors, bound to earth only
by the gravity of our narratives;
and yet, the orb weaver adjusts her snares
with care, each thread a choice in the cosmos,
to capture morning dew or the lost warmth
of yesterday's sun, a gossamer scarf

around the throat of time: and my sister
  steps heavy, laden, her laughter water
on stone—resurrecting forgotten springs:
even as she scolds, her tone a wing
   that grazes my aging ear, asking me
to listen, to embrace the choreography
of days spinning out, the rhythm of change.

www.ingramcontent.com/pod-product-compliance
Lightning Source LLC
Chambersburg PA
CBHW011159090426
42740CB00020B/3402